MW00616967

THE FIELD GUIDE TO
GHOSTS
AND
OTHER APPARITIONS

Other *Field Guides*
to the Unknown

The Field Guide to Extraterrestrials
by Patrick Huyghe

The Field Guide to Bigfoot, Yeti, and
Other Mystery Primates Worldwide
by Loren Coleman and Patrick Huyghe

The Field Guide to UFOs
by Dennis Stacy and Patrick Huyghe

THE FIELD GUIDE TO
GHOSTS
AND
OTHER APPARITIONS

HILARY EVANS and
PATRICK HUYGHE

Illustrated by Harry Trumbore

Quill

An Imprint of HarperCollins*Publishers*

THE FIELD GUIDE TO GHOSTS AND OTHER APPARITIONS. Copyright © 2000 by Hilary Evans and Patrick Huyghe. Illustrations copyright © 2000 by Harry Trumbore. All rights reserved. Printed in the United States of America. No part of this book may be used or reproduced in any manner whatsoever without written permission except in the case of brief quotations embodied in critical articles and reviews. For information address HarperCollins*Publishers* Inc., 10 East 53rd Street, New York, N.Y. 10022.

HarperCollins books may be purchased for educational, business, or sales promotional use. For information, please write to Special Markets Department, HarperCollins*Publishers* Inc., 10 East 53rd Street, New York, N.Y. 10022.

Designed by Stanley S. Drate / Folio Graphics Co. Inc.

FIRST QUILL EDITION 2000

The Library of Congress has catalogued the hardcover edition as follows:

ISBN 0-380-80264-3
00 01 02 03 04   RRD   10 9 8 7 6 5 4 3 2 1

Why *shouldn't* truth be stranger than fiction?
Fiction, after all, has to make sense.
—Mark Twain

CONTENTS

THE FIELD GUIDE TO
GHOSTS
AND
OTHER APPARITIONS

INTRODUCTION

NEWSMAKERS

As we enter the third millennium, the ghost of novelist Ernest Hemingway has been terrifying Cuban employees at his former estate outside Havana. Meanwhile, officials at Madrid's Reina Sofia art museum, which houses Pablo Picasso's masterpiece *Guernica*, have had problems with an apparition named Ataulfo. One guard who went on sick leave to get away from the ghost has asked the Spanish government to investigate. But, as you might expect, the government declined, saying it had "no jurisdiction in paranormal phenomena."

Neither does the U.S. Secret Service apparently. Eleanor Mondale says she was visited by a ghost one night at the vice president's house in Washington, D.C., while her father, Walter Mondale, had the job during Jimmy Carter's presidency. She was so scared by the apparition that she fainted. When she came to, she picked up the "hot line" phone to the Secret Service Command Post and whispered that there was a man in her room. Moments later two agents came charging into her room with their guns drawn. When she told them the "man" was actually a ghost, they told her "never do that again!"

The lesson seems to be that if you happen to see a ghost, don't bother telling any "official" about it. Chances are they won't want to hear it, probably because "officially" ghosts don't exist. It doesn't seem to matter just who the ghost is either, or where they appeared, or what they were doing when they paid their visit. Three Roman emperors—Nero, Caligula, and Galba—reappeared, after their deaths, as ghosts, and centuries later Presidents Abraham Lincoln and James Garfield were both seen in ghostly form at the White House. The ghost of Thomas Jefferson was even heard playing the violin.

Despite the long-standing lack of official interest, however, ghost stories remain very much in the news. They have been told from the beginning of time, and belief in some kind of ghost can be found in every part of the world. The ghost experience is as common in China and Japan as it is in America or Europe, in primitive cultures as well as the most sophisticated. Yet though the ghost experience has been reported for more than 2,000 years, it remains obstinately, defiantly controversial. If you have seen a ghost, you believe in ghosts: Until you see one, you hesitate to believe. And it doesn't help if you look to the experts for guidance. Though the man and woman in the street may accept ghosts as a fact, the scientist remains doggedly skeptical.

The reason for this conflict of attitudes is simple enough: They are not talking about the same thing. The man and woman in the street are talking about the ghost *experience* that they themselves have had or that they have heard about from others. The scientist, on the other hand, is questioning the *existence* of ghosts as physically real phenomena that his instruments will detect and measure. Ordinary people see ghosts in bedrooms: The scientist wants to see a ghost in his laboratory.

In this field guide, we are concerned primarily with *the ghost experience*—with what people say they saw, heard, maybe even smelt or felt. Our book starts from the premise that, whatever form of *existence* ghosts possess, the *experience* of seeing a ghost is real enough. What is illustrated in this book are what men and women like yourself have seen and wondered at. Whether they saw it with their mind's eye, or on the everyday material level, or in some alternative dimension of reality, is another matter. We will offer some thoughts on the matter, but first and foremost it's what people have experienced that concerns us.

IT TAKES ALL KINDS

Though the ghost experience is ancient in form, all along there's been a generally accepted sense, at the popular level, of what ghosts are and what they do. Take Shakespeare. When the ghost of Hamlet's father returns to Earth to urge his son to avenge him, or the ghost of Banquo reproaches Macbeth for his evil deeds, the audiences at the Globe Theatre recognized this as typical ghost behavior. The popular perception of what ghosts look like and how they act has not changed much through the centuries. Ghosts warned, threatened, or advised in Roman days pretty much as they do in our own day.

Today, as ever, the archetypal ghost remains the unhappy spirit of the dead, returning to the land of the living to expiate some wrong committed during its lifetime, or to seek revenge for an injustice of which it was the victim. Occasionally, however, their mission is simply to make contact with those they left behind, to reassure or comfort them. Such ghosts usually appear just once, maybe twice, and then, their mission accomplished, are never seen again. But ghosts also come in many other varieties, as we hope to show.

A particular kind of ghost experience is the "compact" case, in which two people make an agreement that whoever dies first will attempt to communicate with the other. The eminent Italian philosopher Marcilio Ficino died in 1499 after making such an agreement with his friend Mercato. One early morning, shortly afterward, Mercato was studying philosophy when he heard the sound of a horse galloping down the street and stopping at his door. He then heard Ficino's voice saying "Michael! O Michael! Those things are true!" Mercato quickly looked out the window and saw the back of his friend, dressed in white, galloping away on a white horse. Though he called after him, the horse and rider continued on their way. Mercato would later learn that Ficino had died in Florence at the very time of Mercato's vision. There is no record that Ficino's spirit was ever seen again. Having carried out his commitment to his friend, we may suppose that he returned to get on with his new life elsewhere. We may wonder why he chose to appear on a white horse, and so briefly, but it is rather the rule than the exception for ghostly appearances to possess this kind of puzzling, dreamlike quality.

Crises less than death may also serve to bring out the ghost, so to speak, as some mountain climbers, explorers, and others whose activities place them in exceptionally hazardous situations have experienced. In such circumstances, those who experience exceptional incidents seem to take them in stride. An American climbing in the Himalayas was only moderately surprised when he encountered the bartender of New York's "21 Club" who he knew had died five years previously. A British climber in similar circumstances was unfazed when he met two school friends who had died in a motor accident twelve years before. During an unsuccessful 1933 attempt to climb Everest, Frank Smythe was so convinced that he was not alone that he offered a piece of mint cake to his ghostly companion. Travelers at the Poles, solo sailors, and fliers have had similar experiences.

In contrast to those who are just seen once or twice, other ghosts are seen time and time again; they *haunt* a particular place. Some are clearly recognizable as former occupants of the house where they appear, often victims of some domestic tragedy. Others conceal their identity beneath a monk's hood, or manifest anonymously as a "woman in white" or a "man in black." A great many are seen only in the form of a misty wraith. One of the most intriguing of ghost photographs, taken at Rainham Hall, England, in 1936 (see page 41), shows a vague, luminous figure on the staircase. Though it has been tentatively identified as the "Brown Lady" who is associated with the Hall, this is only speculation, for there is nothing to distinguish this ghost from thousands of other shining, spectral shapes.

There have been many animal ghosts, and there have even been ghosts of inanimate objects such as spectral ships seen glowing at sea, giving birth to such legends as "The Flying Dutchman" which inspired Wagner's opera. Phantom armies have been seen fighting in the sky, notably after the battle of Edgehill, during England's Civil War. Only two months after the battle, on Christmas Eve 1642, a kind of replay of the battle was seen in the skies above the battlefield, and repeated several times thereafter. King Charles I, unlike more recent officials, had a Royal Commission inquire into the case and, remarkably, the investigators saw the spectacle for themselves (see page 24).

There are even entire ghost environments. In 1875 Captain Denny, of the Canadian Mounties, took refuge from a storm in a native village which on a subsequent visit he found no longer existed. In 1901 two English teachers, visiting the gardens of Louis XIV's palace at Versailles on the outskirts of Paris, found themselves, so it seemed to them, walking in the ghost of the palace grounds as they had been in the eighteenth century (see page 26). Perhaps these experiences seem to be stretching the concept of ghosts beyond a permissible degree, but Captain Denny's village was full of people—men, women, and children going about their daily activities—were they all ghosts? And one of the two teachers at Versailles saw an aristocratic woman sketching at an easel, and speculated that it might have been Marie Antoinette, the ill-fated queen of Louis XVI.

GHOSTS OF THE LIVING

Despite these exotic variants, the popular image of a ghost remains that of someone returning from the grave, like Shakespeare's ghosts. Nevertheless thousands of ghost experiences involve "phantasms of the living," as the British Society for Psychical Research labeled them in 1886. One of the most dramatic types of case involving a living person is illustrated by the story of a Mrs. Boulton, who for many years had a recurring dream of visiting a particular house. She could describe the place in detail, inside and out, but where it was located, she had no idea. Then in 1883, she and her husband arranged to rent a house in Scotland for the autumn. Her husband went ahead of her to sign the agreement and get the place ready. Upon arrival, the owner, Lady Beresford, warned him that her bedroom in the house was haunted by a harmless "little lady."

When Mrs. Boulton finally arrived, she immediately recognized the house as the one in her dream except for one detail. In her dream, the sitting room led to a suite of rooms that the real house lacked. She later learned, however, that alterations had been done so that the rooms could only be reached from another part of the house. But the biggest surprise took place two days later, when Mrs. Boulton paid a visit to Lady Beresford for the first time. The moment Lady Beresford saw Mrs. Boulton, she exclaimed: "Why, you are the lady who haunts my bedroom!"

Though the "you-are-our-ghost" type of case is generally regarded as folklore, Mrs. Boulton's is by no means the only instance where this kind of double ghost has been recorded with names and dates to authenticate it. The dividing line between folklore and real-life experience is not an easy one to draw in such cases.

An even more worrisome type of living ghost is the *doppelganger*, or "double"—where the witness sees his or her own self. The German poet Goethe tells in his autobiography how he met himself one rainy evening at Weimar, though from his account the apparition was seen with "the mind's eye" rather than the senses. In the 1960s, an American named Harold C., who suffered from severe migraine, saw himself sitting opposite him at the dining-table. In 1951 an English woman suffering from a severe virus infection was visited by her own self, who sat at the foot of the bed, wearing a dress she had discarded a year earlier. Her double advised her about her medication—advice that saved her life.

Phantasms of the living present the greatest challenge to science, for they seem to involve a person being in two places at once. Bi-location is a concept hardly more congenial to scientists than the idea of returning from the dead. But this type of case is entirely compatible with the widespread belief, for which there is a wealth of good evidence, that there is a part of us—often referred to as the "astral body"—which can detach from the physical body and for a short while act independently of it. On occasion the projected self is actually observed by others, at a distance from the physical self.

What is odd, though, about this traveling self is that it is indistinguishable from the real self. When someone who is having an out-of-the-body experience is seen by others, he looks as he normally does, wearing his customary clothes and so forth. In short, it is in no way distinguishable from a ghost of the living, and it is reasonable to wonder if they may be one and the same. But if that is true of ghosts of the living, may it also be true of ghosts of the no-longer-living?

HISTORICAL UNDERSTANDING

It is this kind of puzzling paradox which has made the ghost a source of continuous fascination for scholars throughout the centuries. From the time that ghost stories were first told, it was recognized that they lay outside everyday experience, and required something extraordinary by way of explanation. The history of ghosts is intertwined with attempts to understand them.

The first documented investigation of ghosts is probably that conducted by the first-century philosopher Athenodorus. He was looking for a place to live in Athens when he heard of a house for sale at a bargain price because, the owner reluctantly admitted, it was haunted by a ghost. Undeterred by such things, Athenodorus bought the house and set out to solve the mystery. Late one night, while he was up working, Athenodorus was visited by the apparition—a male figure draped in cloth whose arms were bound in chains. He then followed the apparition and its clanging chains into the garden, where it disappeared. The next day he had the yard dug up where the figure had vanished and there he found a heap of bones—and chains. Athenodorus gave the remains a proper burial and from that day on the ghost was never seen again.

It is clear that, for the peoples of classical Greece and Rome, ghosts were an accepted phenomenon. When in August of 48 B.C., Brutus, on the eve of the battle of Pharsalus, was visited in his tent by the ghost of Julius Caesar, the tyrant he had helped to assassinate, it was acknowledged that the dead Caesar was behaving true to form in haunting his killer. Eighteen centuries later, Lord Lyttelton was visited in 1778 by the ghost of a woman he had wronged and who told him he would die at midnight, three nights later. And this he duly did. "It is the most extraordinary thing that has happened in my day," said Dr. Samuel Johnson of the event, but the case is notable only because it happened to someone so well-known. The person who comes back from the dead to seek vengeance is a classic stereotype of the ghost experience.

Throughout most of history, it has been the priests who have determined the nature of ghosts. In primitive cultures the spirits of the dead are built into tribal religious teachings. It was the same in Europe as long as thinking was dominated by Christian doctrine. To Catholic theologians, ghosts could only be souls temporarily released from purgatory to return briefly to Earth, or apparitions sent by the devil to serve some evil purpose. The ritual of exorcism was devised to encourage the spirit to return, to Heaven or Hell as the case might be.

But Catholic and Protestant theologians could not agree on the nature of ghosts. When the Swiss Protestant priest Louis Lavater wrote *Of Ghostes and Spirites Walking by Nyght* in 1572, he made an all-out attack on the reality of ghosts. He showed how easy it is to misinterpret natural things as ghosts, then he accused Catholic theologians of encouraging the fear of ghosts to inspire awe and reverence among the common people. Not that he denied the possibility of ghosts altogether. But he claimed that any "true" ghosts are delusions fabricated by Satan: "It is the Devil who for the most part is the worker of these things, for he can change himself into all shapes and fashions."

The Catholics were not so dismissive. Though the French lawyer Pierre Le Loyer, in his *Discours de Spectres, Visions et Apparitions* of 1605, agrees with Lavater that many are misinterpretations, and even that some are the work of the devil, he insists that others are spirits of the dead whom God permits to revisit Earth to set a wrong right or to expiate guilt.

It was not until the seventeenth century that a more openminded approach came to be adopted, in which religious doctrines were no longer allowed to dominate speculation. Now, at last, ghosts could be evaluated for what they really were. In *The Secrets of the Invisible World Disclos'd,* the book he wrote as "Andrew Moreton," Daniel Defoe, author of *Robinson Crusoe,* suggested that ghosts could be distinguished as "Angelical, Diabolical, or Human Souls departed." His ghosts generally served a moral purpose, reproaching evildoers like Shakespeare's Banquo, or preventing wrong as when a girl is stopped on her way to an illicit rendezvous by the apparition of her parish priest—an interesting example of a phantasm of the living, and one that could have served President William Jefferson Clinton well.

The turning-point in attitudes towards ghosts was a book published in 1848 by the popular English novelist Catherine Crowe, titled *The Night Side of Nature*. Coincidentally, this was the year in which the Fox sisters in New England were having the experiences that led to the creation of modern spiritualism. But Catherine Crowe's approach to the spirit world took the contrary direction. She considered it a scandal that, all around her, people were having paranormal experiences, yet the scientists did nothing to explain to them what those experiences were.

In 1862 a group of interested Englishmen formed the Ghost Club, an institution which still exists today to share in the serious study of ghosts and other paranormal phenomena, but it was the founding of the Society for Psychical Research (SPR) in 1881 which at last placed research into the ghost phenomenon on a sound, scientific footing. With its definitive studies of "census of apparitions" and "phantasms of the living," it amassed a body of material which has been the basis for all subsequent research.

But even the efforts of the London SPR, the American SPR, and similar bodies elsewhere, have failed to explain the ghost, or even to establish that anything exists outside the mind of the witness who claims to have had the experience. Skeptics insist that there is nothing to be explained, that ghosts are nothing but hallucinations, fantasy creations of the mind, or worse—deliberate creations of the human mind.

HOAXERS AND TRICKSTERS

Because ghosts have such a hold on the popular imagination, there has always been a fondness for ghost stories, fiction as well as fact—and sometimes the fiction has undoubtedly come to be accepted as fact. At times the scam is deliberate. In 1978 the world was told of the horrendous haunting of the Lutz family home in Amityville on Long Island, New York in a book that enjoyed seven months on the best-seller lists. Yet a few years later, the story was revealed as a calculated hoax perpetrated by George Lutz, who hoped to dig himself out of a financial mess.

But most invented ghosts may be created just for the fun of it. The distinguished diplomat Lord Dufferin had a splendid tale of how he was about to step into an elevator in a Paris hotel, only to recoil in horror from an apparition he had once seen years before at a country house in Ireland. When he stepped back and let the elevator go, it plunged down with a broken cable, killing all its occupants. A great story, and he would often tell it as fact, but in 1986 investigator Melvin Harris found it to be pure fiction.

Daniel Defoe had a more kindly purpose in mind when he told how the apparition of Mrs. Veal had appeared at Canterbury in 1705. The story, which is told in the sincerest possible way and with abundant detail, recounts how the apparition of Mrs. Veal appeared to her friend, and in the course of their talk she mentioned Drelincourt's *Book of Death*, which she called the best book ever written on the subject. And well she might, for the entire story was said to have been concocted by Defoe to boost the sales of his friend's book, which had not been selling well.

Since Roman times, the basic rule of investigation has been *Cui bono?*—who benefits? This is abundantly true when ghosts are being investigated. Ghost stories are told, as we have seen, for a multiplicity of reasons, not all of them honest. But even when the ghost itself seems bona fide, our fundamental question must be: Who benefits, the ghost, or the person seeing the ghost?

TESTIMONY AND EVIDENCE

As with so much other paranormal phenomena, the existence of ghosts rests largely on witness testimony, with little evidence to encourage belief that ghosts are "real" in any sense. True, the millions of reported cases cannot be lightly set aside. True, there are a number of multiple-witness cases, when two or more independent witnesses experience the same ghost. But even when an apparition is seen by as many as twenty independent witnesses, as in the Cheltenham case (see page 66), that is not enough to persuade scientists that ghosts materially exist.

Photographic evidence offers the chance of greater conviction, but even photos are easily faked. Many so-called ghost photographs have been exposed as hoaxes, and many more are double exposures, reflections, and other visual artifacts created unwittingly by the camera. Nevertheless, a few photographs have been taken under circumstances which are not easily explained away.

Perhaps the most intriguing of these is the Queen's House photo (cover), which shows a shrouded figure apparently clutching the rail of the famous Tulip staircase (see page 82). One critic claims that a member of the staff, wearing a white coat, rushed up the stairs while the Reverend Hardy and his wife were taking the picture, though surely this is something the couple would have noticed!

The genuine detection of a ghost by a camera or any other non-human instrument would be a major breakthrough. Until that happens, however, it remains an undecided question whether ghosts possess external reality. Is eyesight really involved, or do these apparitions somehow impinge directly on the brain, by-passing the senses while giving the illusion of having passed via the eyes and ears? If so, a blind person should be as capable of "seeing" a ghost as anyone else. The fact that there is no record of a blind person seeing a ghost suggests that they do make themselves seen through the eyes.

It does not necessarily follow that if a ghost can be seen by the eyes, it can be photographed by a camera, though it seems logical that this would be so. Conversely, there are many cases—the Queen's House ghost and the Rainham Hall ghost are just two of many—in which the camera records a ghost even though, at the time the picture was taken, nothing was seen by the photographer.

As always, we are left to face the conclusion that a photograph is only as trustworthy as those who hold the camera. Although it is hard to believe a photographer would not notice someone hurrying across the center of the field of vision, it is just conceivable. And if this is true of the Queen's House photograph, probably the most persuasive ghost photo ever taken, how much more true it is likely to be of any others. Photographs of séance-room materializations, and the "spirit photographs" which were once so popular with spiritualists, have frequently been exposed as deliberate fakes, and those that have not been shown to be the result of trickery are generally unconvincing. In both cases, the "spirit" generally appears swathed in long white draperies. While this may indeed be the clothing favored in the next world, it is also the most convenient kind of clothing to disguise the fact that the supposed spirit is all too human.

As cameras grow more sophisticated, the possibilities for producing fake ghost photographs become increasingly wide. The advent of digital cameras and image editing software offer even further levels of image manipulation. Consequently no photograph deserves to be taken seriously unless every safeguard has been imposed, every test performed, and every circumstance is fully detailed. But even then, it is ultimately a question of whether you trust the witness.

GHOST HUNTING

Those caveats aside, it is worth noting that the images of ghosts captured on film do not always conform to the archetypal stereotype. Often light smudges, glowing orbs, and luminous vortices are all that appear, when no such phenomenon was seen by the photographer at the time the photograph was taken. Skeptics explain these mystery lights as processing errors and errant fingers and camera straps caught by the flash. But ghost hunters like to point out that these light phenomena tend only to appear in photographs of haunted places. When New Jersey ghost investigator Randy Liebeck sent ten such images to Polaroid headquarters in Cambridge, Massachusetts, for analysis, they replied that the images had been caused by electromagnetic fields, or fogging effects due to ionization.

Do ghosts generate electromagnetic fields outside the range visible to the human eye? To answer that question, ghost hunters have begun using ultraviolet and far-infrared films in their cameras, as well as a whole raft of often expensive, hi-tech equipment in their investigations. Loyd Auerbach, a trustee of the American Society for Psychical Research, confirms that instruments have recorded sharply fluctuating magnetic fields—

jumping from the normal background levels of one or two milligauss to as much as 100 milligauss—in places where people see ghosts. These strange electromagnetic fields are usually not static, but move from place to place, and vary in size from that of a basketball to that of a baseball. Perhaps even more significant, according to investigator Liebeck, is the fact that the electrical component of these fields is usually a DC field, like those emitted by mammals and other biological systems, rather than the AC field typical of an electrical circuit.

Meanwhile, portable infrared thermometers have managed to confirm another bit of ghostly lore—the existence of the "cold spots" that sensitive people report feeling where ghosts have been seen. Ambient temperatures may drop as much as twenty to thirty-five degrees centigrade where specters occur, according to Dave Oester of the International Ghost Hunters Society in Crooked River, Oregon. But while ghosts are typically regarded as "cold," some investigators find them to be "hot," at least in a radioactive sense. Using Geiger counters, William Roll, a well-known parapsychologist at the State University of West Georgia in Carrolton, has found signs of radioactivity in the presence of ghosts, as has Liebeck, who claims to have recorded gamma rays from ghosts on several occasions.

This new hi-tech hunt for specters is beginning to show results and these results are attracting the attention of the "mainstream." In his investigations, Bob Schott, the executive producer of *Adventures Beyond,* for example, has been using a night-vision camera that amplifies existing light as much as 70,000 times and records an extra 250 nm of the light spectrum beyond what human eyes can see. While investigating a disturbed American Indian burial ground near the Bell Witch Cave in Adams, Tennessee—the site of a well-known nineteenth-century murderous spirit—Schott's night vision camera recorded an energy pattern emerging from a crevice, according to a story that appeared in the American technology journal, *R&D Magazine,* in 1998. As the light rose, it grew into an image resembling a face. A few minutes later, Schott recorded another cloudlike image. His handheld thermometer meanwhile showed a precipitous ambient temperature drop. Photo and equipment experts who later examined the film, the temperature graph, and the equipment were at a loss to explain how such things could be produced artificially.

Of course, none of this intriguing material is evidence that ghosts are actually spirits of the dead. In fact, for the skeptic, these results are proof of just the kind of freakish natural phenomena that induce hallucinations. But now, at least, it seems there is some agreement about the underlying reality of the phenomenon, even if no one yet agrees just how to interpret it.

THE INVISIBLES

Appearances are not everything, even for ghosts. Some ghosts, as we have noted, are never actually *seen*. The noted American aviator Edith Foltz-Stearns insisted "I never flew alone," for whenever she was in danger, someone—frequently, her dead father—would warn her, saving her from accident on many occasions. Though the aviator never actually saw her supposed companions, she was intensely aware of their presence. Such ghosts, though "invisible," appear to possess just as much reality as those which are seemingly perceived by eyesight or which are detected by the camera. A woman named Margot told folklorist Gillian Bennett how, whenever she visited her widowed grandfather, she would sleep in her old room where, as a child, her grandmother would come in last thing every night to tuck her in. Now that her grandmother was dead, she always had the feeling that she came into the bedroom as she had always done—"not a frightening thing, a good thing, a comforting sort of thing."

The invisible "imaginary playmates" that so many children insist are not imaginary at all, but vividly real, are another such category. In her autobiography, the noted psychic Eileen Garrett recalled hers: "There were two little girls and a boy. I believe that I first met them some time before I went to school, at about four years old. I first saw them framed in the doorway: they stood, as children will, intent on looking: I joined them and after that they came to see me daily. Sometimes they stayed all day, sometimes but a little while, but no day passed of which they were not a part. Until I was thirteen, they remained in touch with me. When I told my aunt and uncle, they were obviously annoyed with me and accused me of lying. They ridiculed the whole idea of the existence of these playmates, yet I touched them and found that they were soft and warm, even as I."

Science would, reasonably enough, dismiss all such imaginary companions as hallucinations induced by stress or distress: for lonely children, the distress of loneliness; for the mountaineer, the stress of the climb. Yet that still leaves questions unanswered. How could Eileen Garrett's hallucinations be so lifelike that she would beg her aunt to come and meet the children for herself? And why, in the case of the climbers mentioned previously, did the hallucinations take these particular forms? Stress and distress may well be the enabling factors, but the ghosts whose manifestations they make possible are no less real, to those who see them, than any other kind.

Most of these unseen ghosts are welcome, bringers of comfort, counsel, or companionship. But there is another type of otherworldly entity whose manifestations are distinctly unwelcome: the *poltergeist*. Some have argued that poltergeists belong in a category of their own, as there is little evidence, if any, to suggest that they are or ever have been human, living or dead. Rather, they give the impression of being mischievous or even malevolent entities, hence their German label which means "noisy spirit."

Today, the consensus interpretation of the poltergeist experience is to reclassify it as RSPK—recurrent spontaneous psychokinesis. The understanding is that the outbreaks originate with the subject, whose mind is the ostensible cause of the activities— the movement of objects, throwing of stones, fires, and pools of water of mysterious origin, and the like. Needless to say, no explanation is forthcoming as to how these things can be made to happen by mindpower alone, but the evidence is strong for associating poltergeists with individuals, usually in a condition of stress, who are—somehow—responsible.

Such physical activities are almost unheard of in connection with ghosts. Ghosts are rarely noisy, and seldom initiate any material action such as moving furniture or throwing objects. Insofar as they display any attitude to the witness, they are generally benevolent. The nearest we know to malicious ghosts are those who haunt a house and seem to regard the witness as an intruder, but even those rarely, if ever, resort to physical violence.

GHOSTS CLASSIFIED

In the strictest use of the term, a ghost is "the disembodied spirit or image of a deceased person, appearing to be alive," according to the authoritative *Encyclopedia of Occultism & Parapsychology*, which specifically excludes apparitions of the living. But hard-and-fast lines are not easy to draw, and the reason for this may lie in a remarkable statement which purports to come from the spirits themselves.

On August 6, 1868, during a séance with the celebrated medium Daniel Dunglas Home, Henry Jencken asked the question "How do you make us see spirit forms?" and got this reply: "At times we make passes over the individual to cause him to see us, sometimes we make the actual resemblance of our former clothing, and of what we were, so that we appear exactly as we were known to you on earth; sometimes we project an image that you see, sometimes we cause it to be produced upon your brain, sometimes you see us as we are, with a cloudlike aura of light around us."

If we can accept this statement, then we are certainly justified in including a wide variety of apparitions in this guidebook under the heading of ghosts. But this has not prevented many students of the subject from attempting to sort them out into categories in an effort to understand them. Some have sorted them by their appearance, some by their behavior, some by their effect on the witness or their ostensible purpose.

The Romans and the Japanese made a distinction between benevolent and malevolent ghosts, though this makes it difficult to classify those "neutral" ghosts which don't give any indication of being either one or the other. The Chinese, though they separated the *shen*—benevolent ancestral ghosts—from the *kuei*—malevolent spirits of demonic nature—recognized that the matter was far from simple. So they went to the other extreme, systematically separating some twenty basic types, with hundreds of subcategories.

Looking at ghosts from a folklorist's perspective, Gillian Bennett perceives a similar distinction between "The Evil Dead"—including hauntings and poltergeists—and "The Good Dead"—including Warning Ghosts. She further perceives a changing pattern, referring to "The Decline of the Purposeful Ghost" followed by "The Rise of the Romantic Ghost." But for folklorists, the focus of interest is not so much the ghosts as the folk who see them, so it is appropriate to ask whether it is the ghosts who have changed or the way we interpret them and their behavior.

The Society for Psychical Research, concerned with the phenomenon rather than its witnesses, made its main distinction between apparitions of the dead and "phantasms of the living." In principle this seems valid, but in practice they had to allow a time margin for what we mean by "living" because, although doctors have their criteria for deciding when a person is clinically dead in body and brain, it is by no means certain that this is true of the mind, soul, or whatever portion of the individual is responsible for manifesting as a ghost.

Others have sought to pigeonhole ghosts by the way in which they manifest. Often, witnesses will describe ghosts as "more real than real." When Canon Phillips was visited by the ghost of writer C. S. Lewis, the ghost sat in the sitting room's other armchair, in front of the television, dressed in his everyday clothes, for all the world as though the man himself had called to pay a visit. By contrast, there are numbers of reports that tell of vague, wraithlike figures which seem to have no substance whatever, and certainly cannot be identified. Clearly there is a world of difference between these two: but is it a difference in kind, or is it simply that the misty ones would do better if they could? Are some ghosts better at being ghosts than others?

Individual writers have introduced their own perceived categories. The distinguished British physicist, mathematician and psychical researcher George N. M. Tyrrell found it useful to talk about four types of ghosts: experimental ghosts, which he defined as the spirits of the living; crisis ghosts, which belong to those who are undergoing some terrible trial, usually death; postmortem ghosts, which appear long after a person's death; and true ghosts, which are the most widely reported, appearing centuries after death, even to those who have no connection with them, but are usually restricted to single place.

Other researchers attempt to distinguish between passive ghosts that resemble mere "tape recordings" and active ghosts that interact with the witness. Above all, there is a distinction that many like to draw between "real" ghosts, those having some kind of autonomous identity, and ghosts which are in the literal sense "figments of the mind." Was Goethe's doppelganger any less "real" because he saw it with his "mind's eye" rather than his sensory eye? Unfortunately, no two people would draw the demarcation line in the same place. The whole question of what constitutes "real" is open for discussion. The fact is, there are no hard-and-fast lines of demarcation, and in this book we have deliberately cast our net widely to include not only ghosts in the strictest sense, but a number of sightings which are "ghostlike" in their manifestation.

The reader may reasonably ask: Does it matter how we classify ghosts? The answer is yes, it does matter, because one of the greatest obstacles to understanding ghosts has been that in the past all the different kinds of apparitions have been lumped together as though they were one and the same. In fact, different types of ghosts present different challenges. For example, when a ghost is seen on many separate occasions by independent people—that surely implies some kind of persistent physical reality. Crisis apparitions, by definition, are one-time ghosts, but they present the ultimate challenge, as they are often seen in circumstances which neither the witness nor anyone else could know about.

The classification system we use here avoids these pitfalls and, we believe, by injecting some order into the encroaching chaos of spectral forms, opens the way to a clearer understanding of the ghost experience.

A NEW TYPOLOGY

Our classification system takes a cue from Camille Flammarion, the famous nineteenth-century French astronomer who also became a notable psychical researcher. In an effort to demonstrate the continuity of existence, he subtitled his "Death and Its Mystery" trilogy, "Before Death," "At the Moment of Death," and "After Death." Good idea, we thought, but the ghost experience is about more than death—it's about time. And so we have ordered our three broadest categories, or classes, of ghosts along a timeline: "Ghosts of the Past," "Ghosts of the Present," and "Ghosts of the Future."

Of the three classes, the **Ghosts of the Past**, by which we mean ghosts of the dead, is the easiest to understand, as this is the traditional meaning of the term ghost. We recognize, of course, that there are several types of postmortem ghosts. The **Revenant**, from the French for "come again," is a ghost who ostensibly returns to Earth from the grave, or from the Next World, or wherever we go after this life. It usually appears just once, or a brief series of times, shortly after the death in question.

A **Haunter**, by contrast, is a ghost who appears repeatedly over time—over years, decades, or more rarely centuries—in a particular building or location. It's as if the ghost has never "left," but stays around, either voluntarily or by compulsion—who knows? In contrast to both Haunters and Revenants are the particularly intriguing **Time Slip** cases that involve not just the apparition of a solitary figure, but its entire set and setting as well. In these cases, it seems as though a whole segment of the past has suddenly come forward to the present, though it could be the other way around. Is it the past that has slipped forward, bringing people of the time with it to manifest as ghosts, or is it the present that has slipped back, carrying the witness with it into the past?

In our second major category, **Ghosts of the Present**, we include both "phantasms of the living" as well as those which occur "at the moment of death." We place these two in the same class for the simple reason that "the moment of death" is not easy to define. Even doctors find it hard to agree precisely when a person can be said to be clinically dead, and from the ghost's point of view it could be that death is spread over several hours, even days. However, if there is a specific unit of time for this category it would be a matter of hours, rather than the days, weeks, months, and years we allow for Ghosts of the Past.

The best-known examples of Ghosts of the Present are what are known as **Crisis Apparitions**. These ghosts manifest in consequence of an accident or some other traumatic incident, not necessarily fatal, but either simultaneous with the event or very close to it in time. The crisis, in our definition of the term, may belong either to the person whose ghost makes an appearance, *or* to the living person who sees the ghost.

While crisis apparitions are somehow intuitively understandable, more puzzling are the **Noncrisis Apparitions** that make up the other major type of Ghosts of the Present. The motivation of such apparitions is obscure; perhaps they are merely spontaneous events. One variety of Noncrisis Apparition is the **Doppelganger** in which the witness sees the "ghost" or "double" of himself or herself. (In some rare cases, this double may also simultaneously be seen by others who are present.) We distinguish these ghosts of the *self* from those of the *other*, by calling those cases in which the witness sees another living person as a ghost or "double" a **Living Other**.

Our third category, the **Ghosts of the Future**, is perhaps most revolutionary in terms of its implications, because these cases seem to defy the most fundamental law of the universe—the inexorable one-way march of time. Yet here we seem to be meeting ghosts coming in the reverse direction—*coming back towards us from the future!* These ghosts have seen that future, and know what is in store for us—that our flight will crash or that a relative is suffering from a fatal disease as yet unsuspected, for example.

The most unambiguous of these time-defying ghosts are the **Harbingers**, those whose only purpose is to convey a warning or an announcement containing information about a future event which we do not possess. These harbingers sometimes take a decidedly inhuman form, the Grim Reaper being the most obvious example. More emphatically precognitive are those **Future Time Slips** that not only inform us about the future but seem to actually take us there, giving us a kind of preview of things to come. There are few such cases in our field guide for the simple reason that they are, by their very nature, difficult to identify. We tend to dismiss anything we see that cannot be identified as something belonging to the present or the past. In order to recognize an event as being of the future, we need the feedback, or confirmation, to occur fairly closely on the heels of the precognitive event itself.

The fifty descriptive cases that follow represent the great variety of ghosts drawn, for the most part, from the vast literature on the subject. This field guide was not designed to be comprehensive, but to illustrate the kinds of ghost experiences people around the world have been reporting for centuries. For the most part, the cases fit quite comfortably within the categories we have designed. Only in a few cases did a lack of case detail force us to push and squeeze a case into one category or another. We should also note that the illustrations that accompany the cases are based either on witness descriptions, other illustrations, or on actual photographs of the ghosts, or of the people involved, living or dead. We have endeavored, as much as possible, to confine the imagination of our illustrator within the known or probable details of each case.

GHOSTS OF THE PAST

TIME SLIPS

CLASS: *Ghost of the Past*
TYPE: *Time Slip*
VARIANT: *Aerial Battle*

DESCRIPTIVE INCIDENT
DATE: *December 24, 1643*
LOCATION: *Edge Hill, Warwickshire, England*
WITNESSES: *William Wood, Samuel Marshall, Colonel Kirke, Captain Dudley, and Captain Wainman, and many others, unnamed*

The battle of Edge Hill, which took place October 24, 1642, was the first major combat of the English Civil War between those loyal to King Charles I and those who supported Parliament. Though the battle was indecisive, Charles, who led the Royalist army, could fairly claim to have defeated the Parliament Army under the earl of Essex.

Two months later, on December 24th, between midnight and one o'clock in the morning, shepherds and travelers in the neighborhood were astonished to see what seemed to be a battle staged in the sky above their heads, including "incorporeal soldiers with ensigns displayed, drums beating, muskets going off, cannons discharged, horses neighing . . ." This continued until two or three in the morning, a total of nearly three hours. The terrified witnesses feared being caught up in the battle and slain if they ran away.

This extraordinary spectacle was repeated the following night, Christmas night, and this time the countryfolk were accompanied by some more educated persons, William Wood, a magistrate, and Samuel Marshall, a minister, who testified to the same event. There were further replays a week later, for a total of about eight "reenactments." It seemed to the observers that the fighting became fiercer with each occasion, so it wasn't precisely the same event each time.

When rumors of the event reached King Charles I, he commissioned three of his officers—Colonel Kirke, Captain Dudley, and Captain Wainman—to investigate. Not only did they confirm the sighting, but they were able to recognize some of their brother-officers in the fighting, including Sir Edmund Varney and others who had been killed in the battle. To all this they testified under oath. The fact that individual participants could be identified implies that this was not only the ghost of a battle, but involved the ghosts of individual soldiers. At the time the general feeling was to interpret these events as a sign of God's displeasure at the Civil War and an urging to make peace.

Inquiries among local residents has revealed a tradition that people have witnessed this spectacle, or at least heard the sounds of fighting, on the anniversary of the battle, up to the present day.

SOURCE: John H. Ingram, *Haunted Homes & Family Traditions* (London: Gibbings, 1897); Antony D. Hippisley Coxe, *Haunted Britain* (London: Hutchinson, 1973).

CLASS: *Ghost of the Past*
TYPE: *Time Slip*
VARIANT: *Park Scene*

DESCRIPTIVE INCIDENT
DATE: *August 10, 1901*
LOCATION: *Versailles, France*
WITNESSES: *Annie Moberly and Eleanor Jourdain*

Two English schoolteachers, Annie Moberly and Eleanor Jourdain, were visiting Versailles, Louis XIV's grand palace just outside of Paris. But as they wandered through the park towards the Trianons, two less grandiose buildings favored by the Royals as private residences, they lost their way, despite the guidebooks they carried. They also felt a strange oppressiveness, which they attributed to the summer heat.

The staff of the park surprised them by their out-of-date costumes, and one man in particular seemed unpleasantly sinister. Moberly was surprised to see a pretty, fair-haired lady in an old-fashioned dress, sitting and apparently sketching. She wore a broad-brimmed white hat, a light-colored scarf around her shoulders, and a low-cut dress with a full skirt. Moberly felt there was something strange about her, but by this time their entire visit seemed to her to have taken on the character of a dream. Later, it emerged that Jourdain hadn't seen the "sketching lady" at all, though it seemed impossible that she could fail to do so. She did remark that the park looked like a tapestry.

Later, upon realizing just how strange their visit had been, the two ladies began to research the palace and its history, and over a period of years they reached the conclusion that, although they had been walking through the park in 1901, they had *seen it* as it had been a long while before, probably in 1789, at the time of the French Revolution. The sketching lady could have been Marie Antoinette herself, and other individuals could be tentatively identified. Not only had they seen people who had been dead more than a hundred years, but they had interacted with them. Many of the buildings they had seen no longer existed, or had been altered. They had even seen figures emerge from doors which had not been opened for years.

Skeptics tend to favor an explanation first ventured in 1965 that Moberly and Jourdain had happened upon a group of amateur theatricals headed by Count Robert de Montesquiou. But, as it turns out, the Count no longer lived at Versailles in 1901. Even if he had, as a man of fashion, he would have made it a point to be as far away from Paris as possible during the scorching heat of August.

SOURCE: Anonymous [Annie Moberly and Eleanor Jourdain] *An Adventure* (London: Macmillan, 1911).

CLASS: *Ghost of the Past*	DESCRIPTIVE INCIDENT
TYPE: *Time Slip*	DATE: *August 1977*
VARIANT: *Dining Scene*	LOCATION: *Hammer Springs, New Zealand*
	WITNESSES: *Allen Kennington*

Allen Kennington was a night porter at the Hammer Lodge, which featured a hot springs and golf course nearby. At 2:15 A.M. early one August morning, Kennington, in the course of his usual chores, was carrying a bucket of coal from the outside into the smoking room, which had been created by dividing the previous dining room into two rooms with a modern glass partition in between. As Kennington pushed open the glass doors, he saw two people he did not recognize sitting at a table. At the head of the old-fashioned, heavy-legged table was an elderly lady in a long gray smock with lace around the neck; a young boy of about twelve, wearing trousers tied just below the knee, sat at the side of the table.

"I just couldn't believe it," said Kennington. "They were sitting there, about seven metres away, like two normal people having breakfast, *but the table was halfway through the wall in the dining room and the portion of the wall where the table was going through was all shimmering—sort of vibrating.*"

The two were eating out of large bowls, breakfast apparently, as there was a toast rack on the table. The woman turned toward Kennington and smiled. He noticed that her face was very lined and there were fresh wet stains down the front of her smock. The boy was about to turn his head toward Kennington, when suddenly "the scene vanished completely!" The frightened night porter then heard a "fearful sobbing just above his head by the chimney."

SOURCE: Robyn Jenkins, *The New Zealand Ghost Book* (Wellington: A. H. & A. W. Reed, 1978).

CLASS: *Ghost of the Past*	**DESCRIPTIVE INCIDENT**
TYPE: *Time Slip*	**DATE:** *July 5, 1991*
VARIANT: *Spectral Army*	**LOCATION:** *Gettysburg, Pennsylvania*
	WITNESS: *Jill Toney*

At 2 A.M. on a hot summer night, the Toney's two-year-old daughter began crying and screaming. Jill Toney hurried up the stairs to find her daughter sitting up in bed quite terrified and babbling "Whatsit. Mommy, whatsit?" Toney heard nothing unusual and managed to get her daughter back to sleep after about fifteen minutes.

On her way back to bed she passed a screen door and stopped to make sure it was locked. While standing there momentarily to get some fresh air, she heard a low noise that grew louder. It sounded to her like people moaning. Several minutes passed and she began to hear a creaking noise on top of the moaning, so she stepped out into the yard to try to see what was happening.

What she saw in the darkness was a line of slowly moving covered wagons with riders on horseback beside them. The moans and groans were now distinct and unmistakable. "That's when I had to admit to myself I was seeing something that couldn't be—I was watching the Confederates retreat from Gettysburg," she later told her husband. More disturbed than scared, Toney watched as the wagons rolled by for three or four minutes. Then they just stopped coming.

Toney later learned that others in the area had had the same experience. She had seen the retreat along the very road where a 17-mile-long wagon train of wounded Confederates passed as Robert E. Lee began his retreat on July 4, 1863. And like Toney's experience, the real retreat had continued through until the fifth.

SOURCE: B. Keith Toney, *Battlefield Ghosts* (Berryville, VA: Rockbridge Publishing, 1997).

GHOSTS OF THE PAST

—

HAUNTERS

CLASS: *Ghost of the Past*	DESCRIPTIVE INCIDENT
TYPE: *Haunter*	DATE: *July 28, 1900*
VARIANT: *Unidentified Person*	LOCATION: *Essex, England*
	WITNESSES: *Elsie, Ethel, Freda, and Mabel Bull*

The rectory at Borley was described by its principal investigator, Harry Price, as "the most haunted house in England," and it remains the best-known and most fully documented haunting in the literature of ghosts. Built in 1863, the Rectory was the scene of uncanny incidents for some eighty years: not only several different apparitions, but also poltergeist events, unattributed sounds, mysterious graffiti, and more. But the most persistent ghost was a nunlike figure, generally seen about dusk, gliding along a path which became known as "the Nun's Walk."

On a summer evening in 1900 Ethel, Freda, and Mabel Bull, daughters of the rector of Borley, were returning home through the Rectory grounds when all three simultaneously saw a female figure with a bowed head. "She was dressed entirely in black, in the garb of a nun," wrote Harry Price who interviewed the witness in 1929. "She appeared to be telling her beads, as her hands were in front of her and appeared to be clasped. The figure was slowly gliding—rather than walking—along the Nun's Walk. She looked intensely sad and ill." They ran to fetch their sister Elsie from the house and as she approached the ghost, it stopped and turned towards her. Elsie stood on the lawn terrified, and the figure vanished.

Ethel, together with the cook, saw the nun again the following November, leaning over the garden gate. Visitors and servants frequently saw her, and in 1927 a carpenter on four occasions saw what he described as a "Sister of Mercy" standing by the gate. The following year a maidservant gave notice after only two days, claiming she had been frightened by a hooded nun at the garden gate.

Who was she? A romantic story tells of a nun whose love affair with a monk from a neighboring monastery ended when she was either strangled by her lover or buried alive by the authorities. During séances held in 1937, a spirit claiming to be the nun, and giving her name as "Mary Lairre," claimed to have been strangled in 1667, but there is no independent confirmation.

SOURCE: Harry Price, *The Most Haunted House in England* (London: Longmans, Green, 1940).

CLASS: *Ghost of the Past*	**DESCRIPTIVE INCIDENT**
TYPE: *Haunter*	**DATE:** *February 1905*
VARIANT: *Black Dog*	**LOCATION:** *North Wales, United Kingdom*
	WITNESS: *Mary Jones*

The religious revival of 1904–5 in North Wales was notable not only for its pious fervor but also for the number of paranormal incidents which occurred in connection with it, many of which were observed by hard-headed, skeptical journalists from London. Most of these phenomena were associated with Mary Jones, a farmer's wife whose preaching was an outstanding feature of the revival. Typically, the manifestations took the form of lights, hovering in the air above the chapels where Jones was preaching, and these were seen as divine signs. But one night she had a more sinister experience.

Returning home, long after midnight, from one of her mission meetings, Jones was dropped by her driver at the head of the lane leading from the main road towards the farm. Her brother always came to meet her when she was late, she told the driver, pointing to the figure of a man dimly seen approaching up the lane. But when the car drove off, the man turned and walked before her down the lane, back towards the farm. She called out to him, calling him by name, and the figure looked back over his shoulder. She then realized it was not her brother at all.

Uneasy, she began singing softly one of the revival hymns. The man suddenly stopped, turned upon her, and became transformed into an enormous black dog, which ran from bank to bank across the road in front of her as though to prevent her advance. Jones thought it was the Devil himself, "angered at my assault upon his kingdom." As she prayed, "he rushed growling into this very hillock," pointing to a solid mound of earth on the side of the lane.

To Jones, Satan was as much a living reality as any of her neighbors, and it came as no surprise to her that the devil would try to interfere with her mission. By singing a Christian hymn, she forced him to show himself as he truly was. Black dogs occur quite often in the folklore of the British Isles, and are generally supposed to be malevolent, a threat or an omen of evil. Generally they seem to haunt a particular location. A similar incident was reported a few weeks later in Abergynlowyn, a neighboring mining town.

SOURCE: Beriah G. Evans, "Merionethshire Mysteries," *The Occult Review*, March 1905.

CLASS: *Ghost of the Past*
TYPE: *Haunter*
VARIANT: *Spectral Ship*

DESCRIPTIVE INCIDENT
DATE: *July 1931*
LOCATION: *Ayacara, Chile*
WITNESSES: *Don Guillermo Vicencio Sanguinetti and unnamed others*

With about 2,500 miles of Pacific coastline, it is perhaps not surprising that one of Chile's most famous ghost legends is that of the phantom ship known as "El Caleuche." The ship is generally described as a schooner of the type used during the last century in the rugged waters of southern Chile's region of channels (where the continent breaks into thousands of small islets), stretching from the island of Chiloe to the Magellan Strait.

Chilean writer Jorge Anfruns located an old seaman, Don Guillermo Vicencio Sanguinetti, who saw the phantom schooner in July 1931 at the port of Ayacara, just south of Chiloe. It was around 10 P.M. on a moonless and foggy night when Don Guillermo and others were at the harbor. "We heard a ship reaching port and dropping its anchor," recalled Don Guillermo. "A few minutes later the fog cleared and a totally illuminated ship appeared, with an approximate length of fifty to sixty meters, and people on deck like in a party. We jumped on boats and rowed to the ship. The sea was calm and we could hear the sound of music and conversation, but just before reaching the ship, a dense fog covered it. A few minutes later the fog cleared and the ship had disappeared." Don Guillermo added that the schooner Lila had disappeared earlier in 1931.

One of the most famous accounts of El Caleuche is that of Raul Torres, Commander of the Chilean Navy patrol vessel Yelcho. "El Caleuche appeared at a distance of about a mile," wrote Commander Torres in the official *Review of the Chilean Navy* in 1940. "We headed at full speed toward the strange ship to attempt boarding. It immediately headed at great speed toward the island [of Huamblin] and disappeared."

The legend of El Caleuche resembles that of the *Flying Dutchman*, which tends to be seen around the Cape of Good Hope. Like the *Flying Dutchman*, whose cruel and belligerent captain, as legend has it, was condemned to sail until Judgment Day, El Caleuche became the curse of the seas and any ship that spotted her would be doomed to ill fortune.

SOURCE: Jorge Anfruns, *Extraterrestres en Chile—Los Testigos Hablan* (Santiago: Editorial El Triunfo, 1996); Héctor Antonio Picco, "La Leyenda del 'Caleuche'—Avistamientos que Preceden a Desapariciones," *Revelación* No 7, June–July 1996; William Brautigan, "Qué Pasa en la Montaña Mágica?" *Revista Contactos Extraterrestres* No 46, Oct. 2, 1978.

CLASS: *Ghost of the Past*
TYPE: *Haunter*
VARIANT: *Identified Person*

DESCRIPTIVE INCIDENT
DATE: *September 19, 1936*
LOCATION: *Norfolk, England*
WITNESS: *Indra Shira*

An apparition known as the "Brown Lady" has haunted Rainham Hall off and on for the past two hundred years. She is thought to be the ghost of Lady Dorothy Townshend, who was the sister of England's first prime minister, Sir Robert Walpole, because the brown brocade dress seen on the ghost so resembles the one worn by Lady Dorothy in a portrait that hangs in Rainham Hall.

Though most of the Brown Lady's appearances occurred prior to 1870, many are well remembered today. She has been—among other things—chased by a Colonel who failed to catch her, and shot at by a Captain whose bullets went right through her. She has also appeared at Houghton, the great mansion built by Sir Robert Walpole, where she once thoroughly frightened the Prince Regent, who later became George IV.

Then in 1936 a camera did what no one else had been able to do. A photographer named Indra Shira had been commissioned to take a series of pictures of Rainham Hall. One afternoon, as Shira and his assistant, named Provand, were taking flash photographs of the magnificent oak staircase, Shira saw "a vapoury form which gradually assumed the appearance of a woman draped in a veil."

As the figure began to descend the staircase, Shira told Provand to take a picture. Shira fired the flash gun and Provand did as he was told, even though he never saw the apparition himself. In fact, Provand was quite amused by the episode—at least until the film was developed. The picture did indeed show the phantom outline of the hooded figure of a woman. The photograph appeared in *Country Life* on December 16, 1936, and caused a sensation. Experts who examined the photograph found no evidence of fraud or fakery.

SOURCE: William Oliver Stevens, *Unbidden Guests* (London: Allen & Unwin, 1949).

CLASS: *Ghost of the Past*	**DESCRIPTIVE INCIDENT**
TYPE: *Haunter*	DATE: *1940*
VARIANT: *Naked Specter*	LOCATION: *Mexico City, Mexico*
	WITNESSES: *G. Frank Clifton and others*

G. Frank Clifton of Brownsboro, Texas, and his young wife were honeymooning in Mexico City. He also planned to do some business while visiting the capital. They were staying at Shirley Courts, part of the Maximilian estates, when something very odd happened.

One night Clifton found himself suddenly wide awake and quite surprised to see a woman he took to be his wife at the foot of the bed. She was kneeling with her arms folded across her breasts. The woman "was nude and her long hair fell down her back," recalled Clifton, which is what led him to believe it was his wife, who, as it happened, had long hair and slept in the nude.

Clifton then sat up in bed, reached out to take her by the arm, and said "Why not come back to bed?" As soon as he did so, however, the naked woman vanished. Clifton then realized that his wife was actually asleep beside him.

The next morning Clifton told the Mexican woman at the desk what had happened to him that night. Did she appear at about two o'clock in the morning? the Mexican woman asked. Yes, replied Clifton. The Mexican woman explained that others had also seen her at about that time. Later, Clifton learned that the caretaker of Shirley Courts had seen the woman many times in an old building they used as a storeroom. This is one of those rare cases where an apparition has appeared without earthly accoutrements—clothes.

More naked ghosts appeared in the Horan Valley, outside of Haditha, Iraq, in August 1999, however. Motorists driving through the town reported that "ghosts appeared next to the bridge, naked and doing some acrobatic moves." The local newspaper said that the "almost human" ghosts were "throwing themselves before cars, causing the drivers to panic."

SOURCE: G. Frank Clifton, "Sometimes 'Minus Britches,' " *Fate*, August 1975, p. 118; Anonymous, "Naked Ghost Scaring Iraqi Drivers," *Newsday*, August 21, 1999.

CLASS: *Ghost of the Past*
TYPE: *Haunter*
VARIANT: *Poltergeist*

DESCRIPTIVE INCIDENT
DATE: *July 6, 1964*
LOCATION: *Beverly Hills, California*
WITNESSES: *Edith Dahlfeld, Joe Hyams, and Elke Sommer*

Just days after moving into their new Beverly Hills home, Elke Sommer, the twenty-three-year-old actress and budding Hollywood star, and her husband, Joe Hyams, a journalist, realized that they were not alone. Elke Sommer was pouring coffee for a visitor, a German journalist named Edith Dahlfeld, when Dahfeld asked if Sommer was going to introduce her to the man. "What man?" asked Sommer, who didn't think her husband was home at the time. "The one who was standing in the hall and just went into the dining room," Dahlfeld replied.

Sommer went looking for the man, who she thought *must* be her husband, but found no one in the house. But Dahlfeld insisted that she had seen a husky man of about fifty with a "potato" nose and hair thinning at the top. He wore dark slacks, a white shirt, and a black tie. The description did not fit Sommer's husband at all.

Two weeks later her mother, who was staying with them at the time, was awakened in her downstairs bedroom in the middle of the night by a man staring at her from the foot of her bed. Before she could scream, however, the man disappeared. In the year that followed, numerous houseguests would report seeing the heavyset man with the white shirt and black tie.

When Sommer and Hyams began hearing strange noises—the sound of dining room chairs being dragged across the floor—every night, Hyams decided to bug his own house. He placed radio transmitters and FM radios connected to tape recorders at the entrance to his driveway, near the front door, and in the dining room, and also marked the position of the chair legs on the floor with chalk. That night, after hearing the chairs move again, he crept downstairs with a revolver in hand and flicked on the lights. No one was there and the chairs were unmoved. And only the tape recorder in the dining room recorded anything unusual: the sound of moving furniture, the flick of a light switch, Hyams's nervous cough, and the sound of moving chairs again once Hyams had left.

Within a year, after two mysterious fires, Hyams put the house up for sale, unable to rid the place of the disturbing manifestations.

SOURCE: Joe Hyams, "Haunted," *The Saturday Evening Post*, July 2, 1966; Joe Hyams, "The Day I Gave Up the Ghost," *The Saturday Evening Post*, June 3, 1967.

CLASS: *Ghost of the Past*	**DESCRIPTIVE INCIDENT**
TYPE: *Haunter*	**DATE:** *March 1968*
VARIANT: *Cat*	**LOCATION:** *Killakee, Ireland*
	WITNESS: *Tom McAssey*

Since the eighteenth century, a large black cat has supposedly haunted the area of Killakee in the mountains of Dublin. A relatively recent sighting took place one evening in March of 1968. The witness this time was Irish artist Tom McAssey. He was painting in the gallery in the Dover House, when one of the two men with him at the time noticed that the door in the old stone hall was open; just a half hour earlier they had both seen McAssey lock and bolt the door shut.

As McAssey walked over to check the outer door, he perceived a "shadowy figure" in the hallway, according to an account published in the *Dublin Evening Herald* in December of 1968. When McAssey called out, "Come in, I see you," a low guttural voice replied: "You can't see me. Leave this door open." The two men who stood behind McAssey heard the voice also, but thought it spoke in a foreign language. Now frightened, the two men retreated.

McAssey did likewise after hearing a "long drawn snore" from the shadow. He quickly slammed the door in a panic and did not look back until he was halfway across the gallery. "The door was open again," he recalled, "and a monstrous black cat crouched in the hall, its red-flecked amber eyes fixed on me." The account doesn't specify what happened next, though presumably McAssey ran and did not see the cat again.

With its image planted firmly in his mind, McAssey went directly to his room and painted the animal exactly as he had seen it. Though monstrous in size, the cat appears otherwise quite normal. Several other people subsequently saw the "black monster," according to the artist. Today, his portrait of the ghostly black cat hangs in the Killakee House restaurant.

SOURCE: Dennis Bardens, *Psychic Animals* (New York: Henry Holt and Company, 1987).

CLASS: *Ghost of the Past*	**DESCRIPTIVE INCIDENT**
TYPE: *Haunter*	DATE: *Early 1969*
VARIANT: *Cemetery Light*	LOCATION: *Silver Cliff, Nevada*
	WITNESSES: *Edward Lineham and Bill Kleine*

For a short period of time in 1880, Silver Cliff, located in the Wet Mountain Valley west of Pueblo, was crawling with some 5,000 prospectors, miners, and those who fed off their bonanzas, all seeking to make their fortune in—what else?—silver. The precious metal soon ran out, however, and the population plummeted to the low hundreds, but not before the dead began to fill the cemetery on the hill above the town.

On the very year the town was established, miners began to report seeing faint blue lights floating above each grave. While these tales were at first dismissed as the fantasies of hard drinking men, in the years that followed many sober citizens would come to witness the same eerie glows in the graveyard.

One of these respectable citizens was Edward Lineham, an assistant editor with *National Geographic* magazine, who in 1969 saw the mysterious lights himself while traveling through Colorado on assignment for the magazine. Bill Kleine, who then ran the local campground and had seen the lights many times before, accompanied Lineham.

On an overcast night with no moon, Lineham spotted the "dim, round spots of blue-white light [that] glowed ethereally among the graves." But as he stepped forward for a better look, the lights would vanish. For fifteen minutes the two witnessed the eerie glows, which also vanished whenever a flashlight was shown at them.

Kleine explained that some people dismissed the lights as a reflection of town lights from Silver Cliff and nearby Westcliff, but to Lineham those small clusters of town lights "seemed far too faint to reflect way out here." Besides, Kleine and his wife had seen the glows when the fog was so thick the towns weren't visible at all.

Still others, said Kleine, thought the glows were produced by the spontaneous ignition of methane from decaying material. Trouble is, the lights were as likely to appear over very old graves that contained nothing but bones, as over the fresh new ones. Local legend, not surprisingly, holds that the lights come from the lamps of long-dead miners, still searching for the precious metal that brought them to Silver Cliff in the first place.

SOURCE: Edward J. Lineham, "Colorado: The Rockies' Pot of Gold," *National Geographic*, August, 1969.

CLASS: *Ghost of the Past*
TYPE: *Haunter*
VARIANT: *Spectral Soldier*

DESCRIPTIVE INCIDENT
DATE: *October 21, 1972*
LOCATION: *West Point, New York*
WITNESSES: *Four unnamed cadets*

Uproars at the United States Military Academy at West Point are normally caused by rowdy living cadets, not silent ghostly ones. But on October 21 an eighteen-year-old cadet of G Company, Third Battalion, Fourth Regiment, saw what he thought was a figure coming *through* the closed door of his ground-floor dorm room. The shimmering, opalescent figure resembled a U.S. cavalry soldier of the eighteenth century, in full uniform, boots, plume rising out of its shako, musket—even a handlebar mustache. By the time the cadet woke his roommate, however, the ghostly figure was already gone.

The next night, however, both cadets in Room 4714 of the forty-seventh Division Barracks *did* see the apparition. This time it walked out of the bureau and stood momentarily in the middle of the floor before disappearing. Then a few nights later, the company commander, Cadet Captain Keith W. Bakken, and another upperclassman commandeered the sparsely furnished sixteen-by-twelve-foot room, and slept, as was customary, in beds separated by a partition. At about 2 A.M. Bakken's companion began shouting, but by the time the Captain rounded the partition, the apparition had vanished. Bakken felt the spot on the wall where the figure vanished and reported that the normally warm wall was icy cold. On a subsequent night, a first classman from the battalion staff spent the night with the plebes and all three saw "a face and shoulder" which "appeared to come out of the wall locker," according to Lieutenant Colonel Patrick Dionne, the academy's public information officer.

A week after the story broke in the newspapers, a midshipman from the United States Naval Academy in Annapolis, Maryland, claimed to have created the West Point apparition using a flashlight, a photographic slide, and a fire extinguisher. But Lieutenant Colonel Dionne said the midshipman's account of how he had pulled off the trick—supposedly the latest in the round of stunts that midshipmen and cadets play on one another at the time of the Army-Navy football game—was full of holes. In an effort to put the story to rest, West Point vacated Room 4714 for several months. Prior spectral appearances at the academy include the ghost of an Irish cook named Molly who is said to haunt the superintendent's mansion.

SOURCE: Robert D. McFadden, "A Ghostly Cavalryman Reports for Duty at West Point," *The New York Times*, November 21, 1992; John Corry, "The Ghost Guard at West Point Gathers Under the Moon (Part 2)," *The New York Times*, November 22, 1972; John Corry, "Navy Calls West Point Ghost Ploy in Old Army Game," *The New York Times*, November 30, 1972.

CLASS: *Ghost of the Past*
TYPE: *Haunter*
VARIANT: *Poltergeist*

DESCRIPTIVE INCIDENT
DATE: *September 1975*
LOCATION: *Culver City, California*
WITNESSES: *Barry Taff, Kerry Gaynor, and dozens of others*

During the summer of 1975, a single mother living with her four children in a shabby, broken down house reported a plague of ghostly manifestations. Most involved a semisolid apparition that was six feet tall. The mother and her eldest son also reported seeing "two dark solid figures with oriental faces," at times struggling with one another, in her bedroom. In addition, the mother claimed that on several occasions she was sexually assaulted by three semivisible beings who left large and distinct black-and-blue marks on her body. The mother, the investigators quickly noted, was an alcoholic who had an emotionally charged relationship with her children, aged 6, 10, 13, and 16.

Over a ten-week period, Barry Taff and Kerry Gaynor of UCLA's Neuropsychiatric Institute visited the home six times to investigate the apparent poltergeist. In the mother's bedroom they noticed spots of "penetrating cold" as well as a strong putrid stench that would come and go. Once Gaynor saw a pan jump out of a kitchen cabinet and follow an elliptical path to the floor. But it was the light phenomenon that dominated the activities in the presence of the investigators.

During some visits, many people would observe "extremely intense greenish-white lights" that varied in size and intensity and lasted for about ten minutes at a time. But attempts to capture the phenomenon on film yielded mixed results. One notable exception occurred when a 35 mm camera operated by an investigator produced a black-and-white photograph of a small ball of light with a faint, cometlike tail. At the same time, a picture taken by a professional photographer on the scene showed a remarkable arc of light over the large group of people in the room. The investigators could find no rational source for any of the light phenomena.

Curiously, during their sixth and final investigative session, "the lights began to take shape, forming a partial three dimensional image of a man, with shoulders head and arms," according to the investigators' report. "More than twenty individuals were present and saw this shape," but the cameras failed to record it. The events of this case were terribly overdramatized in a 1982 movie called *The Entity*.

SOURCE: Barry E. Taff and Kerry Gaynor, "A New Poltergeist Effect," *Theta*, Volume 4 Number 2, Spring 1976.

CLASS: *Ghost of the Past*	**DESCRIPTIVE INCIDENT**
TYPE: *Haunter*	**DATE:** *1976*
VARIANT: *Hand Only*	**LOCATION:** *Hong Kong*
	WITNESS: *Unnamed*

Some ghosts appear to have a tangible effect on the witness and the environment. In this case, the witness was a sixteen-year-old girl. When she awoke, "half sleep," near midnight, she saw next to the wall opposite her a "white shadowy figure." The Chinese saying, *Guai bai kau cheung* ("Ghosts stay near the wall") came to mind.

The witness could not see the face of the figure as it had its back turned toward her. The figure wore a long white robe, had long hair, but had no hands or feet. The girl became very scared and began to pull the blanket over her face. As she did so, she saw "a hand helping me pull the blanket up." It was, she noted, a "*hand only*." She is certain the hand was not connected to the white shadowy figure in any way. She concluded that there must be two ghosts in the room and closed her eyes, not wanting to see anymore.

A few minutes later, she pulled off the blanket, opened her eyes, and again saw the figure by the wall. It had not moved. Then, she told the interviewer, "the hand helped me again as I pulled up the blanket."

When she opened her eyes a third time, the figure was still there but this time when she pulled up the blanket the hand was not there to help. And this time she fell asleep. When she awoke in the morning, there was nothing unusual in her room. The house she was in was "very old," she said, but she had no idea who the apparition might have been.

SOURCE: Charles F. Emmons, *Chinese Ghosts and ESP: A Study of Paranormal Beliefs and Experiences* (Metuchen, NJ: Scarecrow Press, 1982).

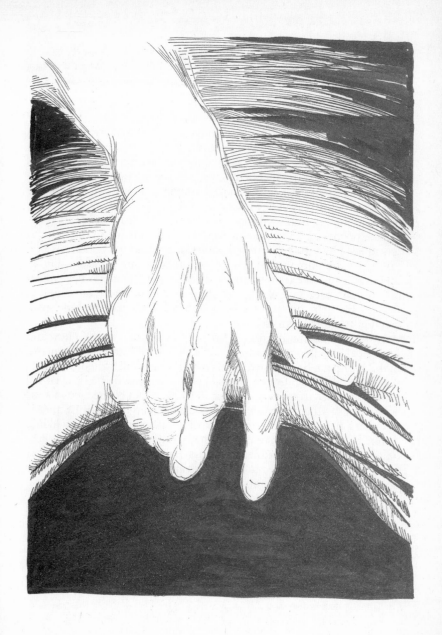

CLASS: *Ghost of the Past*
TYPE: *Haunter*
VARIANT: *Phantom Hitchhiker*

DESCRIPTIVE INCIDENT
DATE: *March 31, 1978*
LOCATION: *Uniondale, South Africa*
WITNESSES: *Dawie van Jaarsveld*

On a drizzly evening South African Army Corporal Dawie van Jaarsveld was riding his motorcycle on the Barranda-Willowmore road to visit his girlfriend in Louterwater. As he listened to the radio through an earphone, he saw ahead of him on the road a brunette in dark pants and a blue top apparently hitchhiking. She was so attractive that when he stopped to pick her up, he looked around cautiously to be sure she was not a decoy for a mugging.

When the girl indicated she wanted a lift, van Jaarsveld offered her a spare helmet and an earphone so she too could listen to the radio. A few miles down the road, the corporal noticed that the rear of his motorcycle was bumping strangely, so he turned around to look—only to find that his passenger was *missing*. Fearful that she might have fallen off, he rode back to look for her, but she was nowhere to be found. Besides, his spare helmet was strapped in its usual place and the spare earplug was in his own ear.

Investigators later confirmed from people at Louterwater Farm and from a café in Uniondale, where van Jaarsveld had stopped that night, that the corporal had seemed deeply disturbed and distracted. Van Jaarsveld later identified from a photograph the woman he had picked up. She was twenty-two-year-old Maria Roux, who had been killed in a car accident near Uniondale in the early morning hours of April 12, 1968.

Others have reported similar experiences in the area, including Anton Le Grange. In May of 1976 he had picked up a young, dark-haired, pale-faced woman wearing dark slacks and a navy blue jacket in the cold rain. She asked to be taken to an address that could not later be verified, then suddenly disappeared from the backseat of his car.

Folklorists cast serious doubts on the validity of phantom hitchhiker stories such as this one, and rightfully so, although this one, unlike most such tales, features real names, dates, and locations.

SOURCE: Michael Goss, *The Evidence for Phantom Hitchhikers* (Wellingborough: Aquarian Press, 1984).

CLASS: *Ghost of the Past*
TYPE: *Haunter*
VARIANT: *Ghost Light*

DESCRIPTIVE INCIDENT
DATE: *August 25, 1979*
LOCATION: *Sarmiento, Patagonia, Argentina*
WITNESSES: *Unnamed soldiers*

In late August 1979, a strange apparition was reported by many soldiers stationed at an Argentine Army garrison in Sarmiento in Chubut province, Patagonia. The stories were collected by Gustavo Fernandez who was then doing his military service in that garrison. The first incident began on the night of August 25, when soldiers at six different guard posts saw the apparition. The sightings continued during the following eight nights. Appropriately, most of them occurred at a guard post in front of a cemetery.

The ghost's shape, however, was geometrical rather than humanoid. Fernandez, who interviewed several witnesses, wrote that "all the descriptions coincided: a shape of a truncated cone, about 1.5 meters high, 'floating' some 20 or 30 centimeters from the ground with a slight waiving motion; it was white but not phosphorescent . . ."

The ghost scared many of the soldiers, who fired numerous rifle shots, although there were no reports that the apparition, anyone, or anything else was hit. Afterwards, the apparition would simply disappear.

The Sarmiento garrison had at the time about four thousand troops, which were on high alert over a territorial dispute with neighboring Chile. The soldiers' jittery nerves over a possible war may have contributed to the ghost stories, but Fernandez discovered there was a local legend about a soldier in 1955 who used to meet his girlfriend at the guard post in front of the cemetery. One night, however, his night watch was changed and he was unable to notify his lover. She came anyway and didn't stop when the replacement guard asked the approaching figure to identify itself. The guard then shot her and the legend says that the ghost returns on moonlit nights looking for her lover.

SOURCE: Gustavo Mario Rodriguez, "El 'Fantasma' de la Guamición," *Revista Contactos Extraterrestres*, No. 84, March 19, 1980.

CLASS: *Ghost of the Past*
TYPE: *Haunter*
VARIANT: *Unidentified Person*

DESCRIPTIVE INCIDENT
DATE: *Fall 1979*
LOCATION: *Old Washington, Ohio*
WITNESS: *Ruth Dixon*

One day in the fall of 1979, Bill and Ruth Dixon were restoring a seventeen-room house they had just bought. Originally built in 1857, the house had first been used as a rest home, then as a doctor's office, so they had to knock down walls that made up the patient cubicles.

When the incident occurred, Bill was in the basement and Ruth was in the parlor with the door shut and the ladder in front of it. From her vantage point eleven feet up on the ladder where she was preparing the plaster for painting, Ruth could peek through the transom and see into the kitchen where the steps to the basement were located. Suddenly Ruth saw a little boy standing in the doorway of the kitchen. "Oh, no," she thought, "Bill must have left the kitchen door open and there's all these paints and dangerous stripper chemicals and things everywhere." So she immediately got off the ladder, moved it aside, and opened the door.

And there, clearer than before, was a little black child of eight or nine. "He wore bib overalls with no shirt and he was barefoot," Ruth told Chris Woodyard, during an interview. "He had a tremendous mop of long curly hair." In his arms was a kerosene lantern so big that it partially covered his face. Ruth wondered where he could have found such a thing.

Then, as she took a few steps toward the boy, Ruth realized she could see through him. "I remember noticing the kitchen cabinets behind him," she recalled. When she took another step, the boy disappeared. A minute or so later, Bill came up the steps holding the bottom of a rusted lantern fourteen inches in diameter, "exactly like the one the child was holding."

Ruth had Bill look all through the house for the boy, but in vain. "He would have had a hard time getting in without being heard," Bill noted, as their noisy dogs would certainly have barked. Later, a search of house records revealed that a prior owner had at one time employed up to four black servants, including a Mrs. Ransom and her son Revedy. The house is also supposed to have been used at the time of the Underground Railroad, whereby runaway slaves were helped to escape.

SOURCE: Chris Woodyard, "The Lad with the Lamp," *Haunted Ohio IV* (Beavercreek, Ohio: Krestel Publications, 1997).

CLASS: *Ghost of the Past*	**DESCRIPTIVE INCIDENT**
TYPE: *Haunter*	DATE: *October 31, 1980*
VARIANT: *Spectral Torsos*	LOCATION: *Kawasaki, Japan*
	WITNESS: *Okuma Isamu*

Okuma Isamu was a fifty-two-year-old fireman with the Kawasaki City Gyokusen branch of the Nakahara Fire Station. At about four o'clock in the morning he was awakened from his sleep in a lower bunk on the second floor. He felt as if someone were pressing against the right side of his chest. He tried asking his colleague to turn on the light, but could neither move nor speak. He then saw a man and a woman staring at him.

The man was in his mid-thirties and had a long, severe-looking face. His upper body was naked and muscular, but he had no legs. Neither did the woman, who was otherwise of average height and build. She wore a kimono and held her round, expressionless face tilted to one side. Then, as suddenly as they had appeared, the two disappeared into the wall. Isamu had had a similar experience just two days before.

After writing an article about his spectral visitations, Isamu learned that many other firemen had had a similar experience there. Of the thirty-two firemen who were stationed at the firehouse at the time, one-third had seen the ghosts. And a year after his article appeared in 1982, Akiyama Mikio, the twenty-five-year-old foreman, saw the torso of a ghost on January 29.

Looking into the matter, Fire Chief Nakajima discovered that the fire station and its twenty-five-meter watchtower had been built in 1959 on the edge of a cemetery attached to the Hottaji temple. Soon afterward a middle-aged woman wearing a white kimono was seen climbing the tower. When the tower was destroyed in 1980, a new building was erected in its place that served as the new sleeping quarters for the firehouse. Several bags full of human bones had been found at the construction site both in 1959 and 1980.

SOURCE: Catrien Ross, *Supernatural and Mysterious Japan: Spirits, Hauntings and Paranormal Phenomena* (Tokyo: Yenbooks, 1996).

CLASS: *Ghost of the Past*
TYPE: *Haunter*
VARIANT: *"Witch"*

DESCRIPTIVE INCIDENT
DATE: *Late 1981*
LOCATION: *Salem, Massachusetts*
WITNESSES: *Barbara Cahill, Dale Lewinski, others*

In 1981, Richard Carlson bought the Joshua Ward House for his expanding real estate business. Ward, a wealthy merchant, had built the attractive brick mansion in the mid-eighteenth century.

One day Barbara Cahill was in the Carlson front office waiting for Sherry Kerr to help her find an apartment, when she noticed a "strange looking woman" sitting in a chair in an office across the hall. The woman's face was almost transparent and didn't look like flesh. She had frizzled hair and wore a long gray coat. No one seemed to be paying any attention to her. When Kerr got off the phone, Cahill turned away and never looked back into that room. Only later would Cahill learn that the house was haunted and that someone would later take a photo of the hag-like creature she had seen that day.

Julie Tache, a Carlson employee, reported that even though she locked her office door every night, sometimes she would come in and find her lamp-shade, wastebasket, or brass candleholders turned upside down, or her desk items and books scattered across the room. She also had a strange choking experience in the second floor room where George Washington had once slept in 1789. Others have also reported a frightening choking sensation in this room. Curiously, the previous dwelling at this location belonged to Sheriff George Corwin, who was known as "The Strangler" during the witch hysteria days of the seventeenth century because of the cruel method he used to gain confessions.

One day before Christmas, realtor Dale Lewinski was taking head-and-shoulder shots of all the Carlson employees with a Polaroid camera. But when she took Lorraine St. Pierre's photo, the camera captured the witch-like hag on film instead. It shows a dark blurry shape with frizzy hair and bony white hands standing in front of a door. One wonders what scenes are being played out here, apparently some three centuries after the original events.

SOURCE: Robert Ellis Cahill, *Haunted Happenings* (Salem, MA: Old Saltbox Publishing House, 1992)

CLASS: *Ghost of the Past*
TYPE: *Haunter*
VARIANT: *Identified Person*

DESCRIPTIVE INCIDENT
DATE: *Mid-July 1985*
LOCATION: *Cheltenham, England*
WITNESSES: *"Randolf Marsh" and "Sheila Brown"*

O ften called the best authenticated ghost of all, the "weeping lady" of Cheltenham continues to weep, even a century after shedding her first tear. One evening in the summer of 1985, just as the street lights were coming on near St. Anne's, "Randolf Marsh," a musician in his sixties and graduate of Oxford, and his friend, "Sheila Brown," were walking on a footpath when they first spotted, about seventy yards away, the figure of a woman with one hand to her face. For about two minutes they watched as the figure, wearing a long black dress of the 1880s with a crinoline, seemed to "glide" along the path. At one point she stopped, turned, and glanced back at the two witnesses. Marsh and Brown hesitated momentarily, then decided to accost the apparition, but she had already disappeared.

The tall weeping lady in black was first seen in a house known as St. Anne's in April of 1882 by a nineteen-year-old medical student named Rosina Despard, who attempted to catch, communicate with, and photograph the entity. On several occasions she set fine strings across the stairs at various heights, but at least twice Despard saw the figure pass right through them. Despard would even follow the apparition into a corner and try to pounce on it, but always the figure eluded her.

Between 1882 and 1889 the apparition was seen by twenty people and heard by others. Since then the sightings of the weeping figure have been rather sporadic, with appearances also occurring in 1956, 1961, and 1970. The specter is thought to be Imogen Swinhoe, who died in 1878 at the age of forty-one. Imogen was the unhappily married second wife of the house's first owner.

In many ways, this convincing apparition is quite unlike most ghosts. The weeping lady is seen not just at night, but in bright sunlight as well, not just briefly, but up to half an hour at a time, and not just indoors, but out and about, in the garden, in the orchard, or elsewhere in the vicinity of St. Anne's.

SOURCE: Andrew Mackenzie, *The Seen and Unseen* (London: Weidenfeld & Nicholson, 1987)

CLASS: *Ghost of the Past*
TYPE: *Haunter*
VARIANT: *Photographic Specter*

DESCRIPTIVE INCIDENT
DATE: *June 4, 1989*
LOCATION: *Madrid, Spain*
WITNESS: *Sol Blano Soler*

The Palace of Linares in Cebeles Square was constructed in 1873. A century later rumors began to circulate that the Palace was haunted, and several researchers set out to investigate its ghostly manifestations. Carmen Sanchez, a psychologist, recorded some strange sounds in the Palace in 1987 and claimed to have been pushed by some invisible force during his investigation.

Two years later, a team headed by a Jesuit priest named José Maria Pilon also produced some evidence of the presences. In some rooms, their instruments registered sudden temperature changes, and in the chapel and the marquis's bedroom, they detected what they believed were powerful psychic forces. Also in 1989, researcher Sol Blanco Soler took more than 450 photographs of the Palace between June and December. Of these, eleven showed strange lights that no one had seen while the pictures were being taken. In one, a large glowing mass appears near a staircase. A laboratory analysis of the photographs concluded that they had not been tampered with but, as in all such photographs, questions arise as to whether a finger or camera strap might not be responsible for the odd "lights."

Why would Linares be haunted? Guesses range far and wide. The site on which the Palace was built was once an olive grove that supposedly harbored bandits. Then in 1808, during the Independence War, the French built a jail on the site and many atrocities took place there. The Palace itself was the original home of the Murga family. According to legend, José de Murga unwittingly married his illegitimate sister who bore him a daughter. When the incest was discovered, the marquis murdered his child and later committed suicide. So the spirits haunting the Palace are thought to be those of father and daughter. In 1992 the Palace was turned into a cultural center known as "Casa de América" (House of America).

SOURCE: Javier Sierra, "Los verdaderos cazafantasmas," *Mas Alla*, No. 57, November 1993; Sol Blanco Soler, "¿Es este el fantasma"?, *Ano Cero*, No. 2, September 1990.

CLASS: *Ghost of the Past*	**DESCRIPTIVE INCIDENT**
TYPE: *Haunter*	**DATE:** *November 8, 1992*
VARIANT: *Spectral Jaywalker*	**LOCATION:** *Blue Bell Hill, Kent, England*
	WITNESS: *Ian Sharpe*

At about midnight, Ian Sharpe was passing the Aylesford turnoff on highway A229 at Blue Bell Hill, when the figure of a young woman ran in front of his car. Sharpe had no time to avoid her, and her eyes locked with his as the car struck the woman then rolled over her. Sharpe quickly stopped his car and, shaking with fear, stepped out into the darkness.

Certain he had killed the woman, Sharpe kneeled down to look under his car, but found nothing. He looked around everywhere, including the nearby bushes, but could not find her body anywhere. After trying unsuccessfully to flag down two cars, he finally decided to drive to Maidstone where he reported the incident to the police.

The police listened to Sharpe, "white-faced and shaking," tell his story and identify the precise location of the accident, before telling him of the legend of the ghost that haunts that stretch of road. The police then accompanied him back to Blue Bell Hill and conducted a search of the area, which proved fruitless. Sharpe's car bore no sign of damage.

Exactly two weeks later, the event repeated itself. This time the driver was nineteen-year-old Christopher Dawkins. He also believed that a woman had run out in front of his car as he was driving on the outskirts of Blue Bell Hill toward Maidstone. The police again found no body and no damage to Dawkins's car.

These incidents have been traced, rather implausibly, to the spirit of Judith Lingham of Rochester, who died along with two girlfriends in a car accident near the top of Blue Bell Hill on November 19, 1965. But more than one apparition may be haunting Blue Bell Hill. In July of 1974 a similar "accident" involved what appeared to be a ten-year-old girl. The most recent series of sightings, in 1993, involve the ghost of a frightful, old woman wearing a long dress.

SOURCE: Sean Tudor, "Hit and Myth," *Fortean Times*, No. 73, February–March 1994; Sean Tudor, "Hell's Belles," *Fortean Times*, No. 104, November 1997.

CLASS: *Ghost of the Past* TYPE: *Haunter* VARIANT: *Aircraft*	DESCRIPTIVE INCIDENT DATE: *May 5, 1995* LOCATION: *Laneside, Hope, Derby, England* WITNESS: *Tony Ingle*

On a sunny afternoon, postman Tony Ingle was out walking the Derbyshire Moors with Ben, his eight-year-old retriever, when shortly before five P.M. he saw a World War II aircraft flying very low, just forty to sixty feet above the moors, and banking to the left. The plane's propellers were turning, recalled Ingle, but they were absolutely silent.

Ingle thought the plane was going to crash and raced 100 yards up the lane as the plane went out of sight. He expected to see the wreckage of the plane in the field, but he found nothing there except "an eerie silence and sheep grazing."

Ingle then called the *Sheffield Journal* in the hope that its newsmen could help him explain the incident. His detailed recall of the plane's appearance enabled him to identify the aircraft from pictures as a Dakota. In researching the incident, the newspaper uncovered the fact that a USAF Dakota had crashed in a heavy mist on July 24, 1945, killing its crew and passengers. This took place just fifty yards from Ingle's sighting.

Subsequently, another hill walker, named John O'Neill, came forward to say that on another occasion he too had seen the Dakota flying at about 600 feet. "What struck me was how slow it was travelling," said O'Neill, "it seemed almost stationary." Then, just seconds later, as he continued his walk, he looked over towards the Mayfield Valley, where he thought the plane was headed, but it had vanished.

There have been numerous sightings of ghost planes in the Peak District "Triangle," which is bound by Glossop to the west, Sheffield to the east, and Buxton to the south. More than 300 people lost their lives in more than fifty air crashes in the area during and since World War II. The latest phantom plane incident occurred on March 24, 1997, when so many people reported that a strange, low-flying prop plane was about to crash that a full-scale search operation was undertaken with two helicopters and more than 250 men. Nothing was ever found.

SOURCE: "Ghost Plane Mystifies Postman," *Fortean Times*, No. 82, Aug.–Sept. 1995; "Ghost Bomber Runs," *Fortean Times*, No. 100, July 1997.

CLASS: *Ghost of the Past*	DESCRIPTIVE INCIDENT
TYPE: *Haunter*	DATE: *November 1995*
VARIANT: *Photographic Specter*	LOCATION: *Scappoose, Oregon*
	WITNESSES: *Micky Scholl, Dave Oester, Sharon Gill*

D oug Sellers is the owner of the Sellers Arts and Craft store, located on the Columbia River Highway north of Portland. He never believed in ghosts until he moved into the apartment above the store. First he would find things—a ribbon display box or paint can—that were out of place. His cat, Skimbles, started acting strangely, too, hiding out in the back of a closet. And one day Sellers felt something cold brush against his cheek as he was talking on the phone.

Then Micky Scholl saw *it*. She was putting away bags of Pogs, or milk caps, in the warehouse section of the second floor, when she heard a sound over in the next aisle. When she turned the corner to find out who it was, she saw a white misty apparition, threw up her hands, screamed, and the milk caps landed all over the floor.

At that point Sellers decided to call in Dave Oester and Sharon Gill, a pair of ghost hunters and professional photographers who lived nearby, to investigate. Using a gaussmeter, which registers deviations in the magnetic field, they headed up the aisle where Micky had seen the apparition and found on top of a broom box on the top shelf a magnetic variation that was 500 times greater than the normal background. The strange energy field was about the size and shape of a football and remained there for twenty minutes before vanishing completely.

A few days later Oester and Gill picked up from the developing lab the photographs they had shot at Sellers Arts and Crafts during their investigation. One photograph, taken from the top of the stairs looking down, surprised them. On it was "a swirling tornado-like energy vortex" that cast a shadow on the opposite wall, even though the vortex had been invisible to the naked eye.

Could it have been their camera strap? Oester, a professional photographer, denies this: "We always wear it around the wrist to avoid dropping the [expensive] camera." They have since obtained more of these "vortex" light images at funerals, cemeteries, and other haunted places. They believe that our bodies at death can assume a variety of electromagnetic forms, such as balls of light, vortexes, mists, and other spectral shapes.

SOURCE: Sharon A. Gill and Dave R. Oester, *The Haunted Reality: True Ghost Tales* (St. Helens, OR: StarWest, 1996).

GHOSTS OF
THE PAST

REVENANTS

CLASS: *Ghost of the Past*	**DESCRIPTIVE INCIDENT**
TYPE: *Revenant*	**DATE:** *November 30, 1860*
VARIANT: *Simultaneous Specters*	**LOCATION:** *Kashin, Russia*
	WITNESSES: *Basil von Driesen and Basil Bajenoff*

Between 1 and 2 o'clock in the morning Baron von Driesen put down the Bible he was reading and prepared to go to sleep. Just as he snuffed out the candle, he heard the sound of slippers shuffling in the next room. "Who is there?" he called out. There was no answer.

The Baron struck several matches in an attempt to relight the candle when suddenly he saw his father-in-law, Nicholas Ponomareff, who had died nine days earlier, standing at the closed door. The Baron had not been on good terms with Ponomareff, whose departed soul was to be celebrated in a liturgy later that day.

"What do you want?" asked the baron. Ponomareff was wearing his blue dressing gown lined with squirrel fur. Since it was only half buttoned, the baron could see Ponomareff's white waistcoat and black trousers underneath.

Ponomareff stepped forward and stopped at the baron's bed. "Basil Feodorovitch," said the ghost, "I have acted wrongly towards you. Forgive me! Without this I do not feel at rest there." The ghost of Ponomareff pointed to the ceiling with his left hand and held out his right hand to the baron.

Von Driesen grabbed the long, cold hand and shook it, saying: "God is my witness that I have never had anything against you." The ghost then bowed, and went out through the opposite door into the billiard room, and disappeared. Von Driesen crossed himself, put out the candle, and fell asleep.

After the service later that day, the priest, Reverend Basil Bajenoff, admitted to the baron and his wife that Ponomareff had also appeared to him the previous night at the same time and begged him to reconcile him with his son-in-law. On July 23, 1891, the priest signed a written statement to that effect. The investigators were impressed by the fact that the case involved a ghost that appeared simultaneously to two people in different locations.

SOURCE: Sidgwick Committee, "Report on the Census of Hallucinations," *Proceedings of the Society for Psychical Research*, Vol. X (London: Kegan Paul, Trench, Trübner and Co., 1894).

CLASS: *Ghost of the Past*
TYPE: *Revenant*
VARIANT: *Faces Only*

DESCRIPTIVE INCIDENT
DATE: *December 5, 1924*
LOCATION: *Pacific Ocean*
WITNESSES: *Captain Keith Tracy and crew of SS* Watertown

Tragedy struck the S.S. *Watertown,* a large oil tanker, as it cruised down the California coast on the way to New Orleans via the Panama Canal. In the process of cleaning a cargo tank, two sailors, James Courtney and Michael Meehan, were overcome by fumes and died. On the fourth of December their bodies were buried at sea off the Mexican coast.

Just before dusk the following day, the first mate reported seeing the two faces of the dead men in the waves near the ship. The ghostly heads continued to appear while the ship sailed the Pacific and many in the crew, including Captain Keith Tracy, were witness to the eerie phenomenon.

Invariably the two heads would appear about ten feet apart and about forty feet from the ship, floating on the crest of the waves. Always larger than living heads, the apparition would last about ten seconds before fading then reappearing. Once the ship reached the Atlantic, however, the heads were no longer seen.

On arrival in New Orleans, Captain Tracy reported the event to the shipping office—the Cities Service Company. The company's J. S. Patton suggested that they try to photograph the faces and on the next cruise, the first mate brought along a camera. When the apparitions appeared again, Tracy photographed the faces then locked the camera and film in his safe. When the film was developed by a commercial developer, five of the six exposures revealed nothing unusual, but one showed the faces quite distinctly.

On the third voyage, the faces appeared less frequently, and subsequently the ship's crew changed and there were no more reports of the ghostly faces. Some crewmen believed the apparition was an optical effect and the identification with the dead sailors was simple suggestion. But optical effects are unlikely to recur day after day and be seen by such large numbers of people.

SOURCE: D. Scott Rogo, *An Experience of Phantoms* (New York: Taplinger, 1974).

CLASS: *Ghost of the Past*
TYPE: *Revenant*
VARIANT: *Photographic Specter*

DESCRIPTIVE INCIDENT
DATE: *June 19, 1966*
LOCATION: *Greenwich, England*
WITNESS: *Reverend and Mrs. R. W. Hardy*

While on holiday in England, the Reverend and Mrs. R. W. Hardy, of White Rock, British Columbia, visited the Queen's House, which Charles I built for his queen, Henrietta Maria, on the Thames below London. At about five o'clock in the afternoon, during the museum's normal operating hours, the Reverend took a series of photographs, including one of the magnificent Tulip staircase. Upon returning to Canada, the Hardys had their photographs developed and, to their surprise, one showed a shrouded figure apparently clutching the rail of the famous stairway. The pictures before and after on the film show other parts of the Museum, but nothing even remotely resembles either the shrouded figure or the staircase.

In recalling that her husband had taken the photograph, Mrs. Hardy stated: "Thus I was free to watch for any possible intrusion of anything visible during the exposure time. Actually, a group of people who noticed our preparation apologized and stepped back, although I explained that my husband was not quite ready . . . no person or visible object could have intervened without my noticing it. We had tried to ascend the staircase but were blocked by a 'No Admittance' sign and a rope barrier at the foot of the stairs."

On first examination the picture (see cover) appears to show a single figure, with an exceptionally long right hand reaching ahead of the figure. But closer scrutiny establishes that both the hands on the stair rail are left hands; both also display a ring on the marriage finger. The "top" shadow figure is oddly convincing since the shadow falls directly across the light rays emitted by the electric candelabra. The lower shrouded figure is leaning forward, apparently in pursuit of the "shadow" figure as they ascend the stairs.

Kodak and other photographic experts concluded that the transparency had not been manipulated. The only logical explanation is that there must have been someone on the stairs. But the Hardys explicitly stated otherwise, and the museum warders are very strict about not letting people up on the staircase. They would certainly not countenance any dressing-up or playing about in the Queen's House. Brian Termain, the senior museum photographer, reportedly used yards of film trying, unsuccessfully, to reproduce the effects in the Hardys' picture.

SOURCE: Peter Underwood, *A Host of Hauntings* (London: Leslie Frewin, 1973).

CLASS: *Ghost of the Past*
TYPE: *Revenant*
VARIANT: *Protective Pilot*

DESCRIPTIVE INCIDENT
DATE: *June 1972*
LOCATION: *Newark, New Jersey*
WITNESSES: *Sis Patterson, Diane Boas, and an unnamed flight captain*

On Friday, December 19, 1972, Eastern Airlines Flight 401 from New York to Miami crashed in the Florida Everglades. One hundred passengers and crew members lost their lives, including Bob Loft, the captain of the Lockheed L-1011, and second officer Dan Repo, the flight engineer. An investigation found that the crew had become so preoccupied with a landing gear malfunction that they failed to realize the extent of the aircraft's descent before it was too late.

Within a month of the crash, Eastern crews began experiencing cold sensations and invisible presences aboard L-1011s. Most of the incidents occurred on Eastern plane number 318, though some came from other L-1011s Eastern had leased to other airlines. One feature seemed to link these planes—all had received parts salvaged from the crash of Flight 401.

The most striking encounter took place aboard Eastern plane number 318 as it stood at the gate at Newark Airport in June 1972. In preparation for takeoff, Sis Patterson, the senior stewardess, made a head count and discovered she had one person more aboard than the passenger list indicated. In double-checking, she found that the extra passenger was an Eastern captain in uniform sitting in first class. This in itself was not unusual as pilots deadheading back to their point of origin would often ride in first class for the first part of the trip.

But when Patterson went up to the captain and inquired whether he was jump-seat riding this trip, she received no reply. The captain simply stared straight ahead. When she asked a second time, the captain said nothing. A moment later, Diane Boas, the flight supervisor, joined Patterson, and she too was puzzled by the man's unresponsiveness. The captain appeared normal, but seemed to be in a daze.

Worried, Paterson fetched the flight captain from the cockpit. A half-dozen other passengers sat in the vicinity of the deadhead captain. When the flight captain approached and leaned down to address the other captain, he cried out: "My God, it's Bob Loft!" The cabin went silent. One moment the captain in the first class seat was full-bodied and solid, the next moment he had vanished. A long delay followed, during which the plane was searched, but the missing captain could not be found, and finally the plane took off for Miami.

In all, more than two-dozen such incidents were reported aboard the L-1011s, reaching a peak in June 1973 and ending suddenly in the spring of 1974. Bob Loft's ghost appeared more often early on. Dan Repo's ghost seemed particularly concerned with the safety of the planes on which he was seen. Several times he is said to have either fixed or warned the crew of a problem. The log sheets containing these sighting reports were missing from the aircraft's log books, but the reports were so widely circulated throughout the aviation community that Eastern is said to have eventually removed all parts associated with Flight 401 from its planes.

SOURCE: John G. Fuller, *The Ghost of Flight 401* (New York: Berkley, 1976).

CLASS: *Ghost of the Past*
TYPE: *Revenant*
VARIANT: *War Victim*

DESCRIPTIVE INCIDENT
DATE: *December 1995*
LOCATION: *Tuzla, Bosnia*
WITNESSES: *Mustafa Piric*

On May 25, 1995, a mortar attack by Bosnian Serbs killed seventy-one people in Kapija Square in Tuzla's old town. Many people lost their legs or arms or were decapitated. For months after the tragedy the square remained largely deserted at night, as people heard strange sounds and moans coming from it. Word spread that a young woman who died in the blast haunted the place in a vain search for her severed legs.

A military police officer named Mustafa Piric supposedly spotted the ghost of the young woman in December. It was after curfew and Officer Piric had stopped a girl with long, blond hair to ask to see her identification papers. When the young woman turned around, Piric was shocked to find that she had no face. She then cried "Give me back my legs!" and presumably disappeared, though the report does not say so explicitly. Three other police officers have also reported seeing the ghost of the girl while on patrol, according to a nurse named Maida Mamzic.

"A lot of people here believe in ghosts and spirits," said Alma Ahmedbegovic, a twenty-year-old radio reporter. "They believe this girl's spirit can't rest because she was buried without her legs."

Apparitions are common in war zones. Many of the people in Tuzla have supposedly awoken from their nightmares only to find their dead friends standing in front of them.

SOURCE: "Legless ghost has Bosnians spooked in Tuzla bombsite," *Fortean Times*, No. 87, June 1996.

GHOSTS OF THE PRESENT

CRISIS APPARITIONS

CLASS: *Ghost of the Present*	**DESCRIPTIVE INCIDENT**
TYPE: *Crisis Apparition*	**DATE:** *July 1895*
VARIANT: *Historical Figure*	**LOCATION:** *Atlantic Ocean, between the Azores and Gibraltar*
	WITNESS: *Captain Joshua Slocum*

In the summer of 1895, veteran sailor Captain Joshua Slocum was completing the first leg of the voyage which earned him his place in history as the first person to sail alone round the world. Between the Azores and Gibraltar his rugged but tiny sloop *Spray* ran into squalls. At the same time, Slocum was suffering from severe stomach cramps which so demoralized him that he went below, not taking in his sails as he knew he should, and threw himself on the cabin floor in agony. He lost track of how long he lay there, for he became delirious.

When Slocum came to, he realized that his sloop was plunging into a heavy sea. Looking out of the companionway, to his amazement he saw a tall man at the helm. His rigid hand, grasping the spokes of the wheel, held them as in a vise. He was dressed like a foreign sailor, with a large red cap over his left ear, and sporting shaggy black whiskers. Slocum wondered if this alarming personage, the very image of a pirate, had boarded his boat and planned to cut his throat.

The sailor seemed to read his thoughts, for he doffed his cap to Slocum, saying, with the ghost of a smile "Señor, I have come to do you no harm. I am one of Columbus's crew, the pilot of the *Pinta,* come to aid you. Lie quiet, señor captain, and I will guide your ship tonight. You have a *calentura* [a reference to the stomach cramps] but you will be all right tomorrow . . . You did wrong to mix cheese with plums."

Next day Slocum found that the *Spray* was still heading as he had left her, and felt that "Columbus himself could not have held her more exactly on her course." That night he received a second visit from the Spanish sailor, but this time it was in a dream. He explained that he would like to sail with Slocum on his voyage, for the love of adventure alone. Then, doffing his cap, he disappeared as mysteriously as he had arrived.

Slocum woke with the feeling that he had been in the presence of a friend and a seaman of vast experience. And though he recognized his second sighting as a dream, he also realized that the first had been something altogether different. Besides, what dream could hold a vessel on course through a violent sea?

SOURCE: Joshua Slocum, *Sailing Alone Around the World* (New York: Dover, 1978).

CLASS: *Ghost of the Present*	DESCRIPTIVE INCIDENT
TYPE: *Crisis Apparition*	DATE: *Between 1915 and 1918*
VARIANT: *Living Other*	LOCATION: *Hobart, Tasmania, Australia*
	WITNESS: *Ruth Taylor*

D uring World War I army nursing sisters like Ruth Taylor served on troopships returning the wounded to Australia. Taylor received her training as a nurse at Hobart Hospital. During her second year of training a "little incident" took place while she was in charge of night duty on the men's medical floor.

When she reported for duty at 9 P.M., the day-sister gave her special instructions regarding a young Irish sailor at the end of Ward 5: "He was brought in today from HMS *Bellerophon,* a very sick boy, and I fear that he may already be beyond human aid; watch him closely and try to give his treatment regularly. He has not spoken at all . . ."

At about 9:20 P.M. Taylor was halfway through Ward 5, making her way from bed to bed, when suddenly she noticed "a beam of clear moonlight" shining upon the bed occupied by the Irish sailor. "Kneeling beside him," said Taylor, "was a little old lady in black" with a "red rose in her old-fashioned bonnet." Taylor stood watching as tears ran down the old woman's wrinkled cheeks, though most of her face was in shadow. The woman held the sailor's hand in her own old worn hand. He was still except for his labored breathing. Taylor was surprised by this scene since the day-sister had not mentioned that he had any family here.

As Taylor walked toward them, however, the old woman began fading away, until at the sailor's bedside, there was no sign of her. Taylor saw the sailor's eyes open so she asked: "How are you, Flynn?" He replied: "Better nurse. I've just had a lovely dream about my old mother." Taylor was shaken by his remark, but thought better about mentioning what she had just seen. Through the night, the sailor repeated the word *Mother* in his soft Irish brogue as he slept.

In the morning, Taylor told one of the day nurses to ask the sailor, who would eventually recover, about his dream. She did and "he told her that he had dreamed that his mother had kneeled beside him, cried over him and begged him to come home." The details tallied exactly with what Taylor had seen, down to the red rose in her bonnet.

SOURCE: Frank Cusack (ed.), *Australian Ghost Stories* (Melbourne: William Heinemann Ltd, 1967).

CLASS: *Ghost of the Present*	DESCRIPTIVE INCIDENT
TYPE: *Crisis Apparition*	DATE: *June 11, 1923*
VARIANT: *Relative at Death*	LOCATION: *Indianapolis, Indiana*
	WITNESS: *Gladys Watson*

In a preamble to her account, Watson, who was the daughter of a Methodist minister, noted that she had been "schooled against superstition." When the out-of-the ordinary incident occurred, Watson was pregnant and looking forward to showing off her new addition to her family in Wilmington, Delaware, where her grandfather lived with her mother and father.

On the night in question, after sleeping for about three or four hours, Watson awoke when she heard someone calling her name. When she sat up in bed, she saw her grandfather standing near the foot of the bed, leaning in towards her somewhat. His figure was illuminated by light shining in the window from the Lilly Laboratory next door.

"Don't be frightened," said her grandfather in a soft but determined voice, "it's only me. I have just died." Watson started crying and reached out across the bed to wake her husband. "This is how they will bury me," the grandfather, who was dressed in a black bow tie, continued. "I just wanted to tell you that I've been waiting to go ever since Ad was taken." Ad was Adaline, Watson's grandmother who had been dead for several years.

When her husband awoke, he asked what was the matter. She explained that her grandfather had just been there and that he had just died. Her husband thought it was all just a nightmare, as her grandfather, despite his advanced age, was in very good health at the time. When Watson insisted that he had died, her husband went down to the public telephone on the corner at 4:05 A.M. and called her parents' home.

Watson's mother, who had been up most of the night, was surprised by the call. But, yes, Granddad, who had taken sick suddenly the day before, had just died. An investigation of the precise timing of the events revealed that the grandfather had been dead less than thirty minutes when he appeared at the foot of his grandchild's bed.

SOURCE: L. A. Dale, "A Series of Spontaneous Cases in the Tradition of *Phantoms of the Living*," *The Journal of the American Society for Psychical Research*, Vol. 45, No. 3, July 1951.

CLASS: *Ghost of the Present*
TYPE: *Crisis Apparition*
VARIANT: *Ghost Light*

DESCRIPTIVE INCIDENT
DATE: *1950s*
LOCATION: *Bavarian Alps, Germany*
WITNESS: *Frau Elsa Schmidt-Falk*

Elsa Schmidt-Falk, a German officer's widow, had a remarkable experience while climbing alone in the Bavarian Alps. The mountain she was on was not notably dangerous, provided one kept to the regular "tourists' route." Unfortunately, her climb had taken her longer than expected, and by the time she commenced her return, the light was already beginning to fade.

All of a sudden she realized that she had strayed from the path and she found herself in danger. In fact, a year later a young girl would fall to her death in precisely the same place. Suddenly Schmidt-Falk became aware of what she described as "a sort of a big ball of light," which condensed to the shape of a tall, rather Chinese-looking gentleman. She was neither surprised nor astonished by the apparition: at the time it all seemed quite natural.

The mysterious gentleman bowed to her, spoke a few reassuring words, then led her back to the tourists' path and disappeared in the same remarkable way as he had appeared, condensing into a ball of light that then vanished. She made her way safely to the foot of the mountain.

Though easily dismissed as nothing more than a hallucination induced by the stress of finding herself in a life-or-death situation, one wonders what kind of hallucination it is that can rescue an individual from a perilous situation? Where did the knowledge of the correct route come from? Insofar as it provided a very real answer to a very real crisis, Frau Schmidt-Falk's oriental entity has more in common with guardian angels than traditional haunting specters.

Interestingly, the phenomenon of a figure materializing from a small luminous source has been reported in other contexts. A notable example was reported by Nobel scientist Charles Richet, who, while investigating phenomena at the Villa Carmen, Algiers, saw something resembling a white handkerchief lying on the ground, which gradually shaped itself into a full-size human figure.

SOURCE: Personal correspondence, letter to Hilary Evans, January 27, 1959; Charles Richet, *Traité de Métapsychique* (Paris: Felix Alcan 1922), p. 647.

CLASS: *Ghost of the Present*
TYPE: *Crisis Apparition*
VARIANT: *Death Message*

DESCRIPTIVE INCIDENT
DATE: *November 15, 1958*
LOCATION: *Over the United States*
WITNESS: *Vincent Price*

The 1953 three-dimensional movie *House of Wax* made a star of Vincent Price. Thereafter he was typecast as the screen's most suave merchant of menace. Several years before his death in 1993 the actor told journalist and author Michael Mumm an odd story of how he had learned of the death of a good friend and fellow actor.

Price had been on a plane, flying from Hollywood to New York, when he glanced up from the classic French novel he was reading to look out the window. And there, emblazoned on a cloudbank, were the letters TYRONE POWER IS DEAD, "like a giant teletype that was lit up with brilliant light that came from within the clouds."

At first Price thought he might be seeing things as no one else on the airplane acted as if they had seen the words. But he was certain that he had seen the words and swore to the journalist that this had happened.

After landing in New York, Price learned that while his plane had been in the clouds, Tyrone Power had died of a heart attack on the set of *Solomon and Sheba* in Spain. Price was convinced that he had not imagined the episode, as he had no idea Power was going to die. He regarded the words as "a message sent by Ty."

SOURCE: Vincent Price, "In the Clouds," *Dancing with the Dark*, Stephen Jones (ed.) (London: Vista, 1997).

CLASS: *Ghost of the Present*	**DESCRIPTIVE INCIDENT**
TYPE: *Crisis Apparition*	**DATE:** *1974*
VARIANT: *Grim Reaper with scythe*	**LOCATION:** *Yonkers, New York*
	WITNESS: *A.L.*

At about 10:15 one night, the witness, known only as A.L., was lying down on the sofa in the living room of his apartment. His wife and children were asleep. Suddenly, a strange feeling came over him, as if someone were watching him. Glancing to his right, he saw, standing at his side, a figure holding a scythe upright. "He wore a black hooded robe," A.L. wrote in a letter to investigator Mark Chorvinsky. "His face was a gleaming white skull."

Gripped with fear, A.L. blurted out: "Who sent you to me? Go back to where you came from." Slowly the reaper figure glided backward, never turning his back on A.L., and finally vanished through the closed front door. A.L., having recognized the figure as the grim reaper, wondered momentarily why he was still alive, then realized that the reaper may have come for someone else in his family.

A.L. immediately ran to the bathroom, where he found his wife "out cold." On the bed was an empty bottle of sleeping pills. He tried hard to wake her, but was unsuccessful, so he decided to get help and called his sister who lived nearby. She came over with her husband and the three spent hours walking A.L.'s suicidal wife around the apartment. Finally, they took her to the hospital. A week later, she was released and, as A.L. wrote, "we went on with our lives."

Though folklore generally regards the reaper as "a taker of souls," in A.L.'s case, he was simply an omen in which death was a possible outcome. Not so oddly perhaps, A.L. now considers the reaper "a special friend."

SOURCE: Mark Chorvinsky, "Our Strange World," *Fate*, July 1992.

CLASS: *Ghost of the Present*
TYPE: *Crisis Apparition*
VARIANT: *Living Other*

DESCRIPTIVE INCIDENT
DATE: *1977*
LOCATION: *East Anglia, England*
WITNESS: *Shirley Gray*

Early one morning Shirley Gray was awakened by a voice calling out her name. When she opened her eyes, Gray saw the head and shoulders of her friend Pat Craven hovering over the foot of her bed. Though Craven appeared in distress, what struck Gray were the strange clothes she was wearing. Gray knew Craven as a stylish dresser, but here she was in a shabby, square-cut garment with a ragged neckline—clothes she would not normally be caught dead in, as the saying goes.

When she got up, Gray tried to contact Craven, but learned that she was away on vacation in Kenya. Oddly enough, Gray and Craven were not particularly close friends, merely "Christmas-card friends." But the incident had disturbed Gray enough that she tried to call Craven every day for a week. When Gray finally reached her, Craven had just returned from her trip hours before. The first thing Gray said was: "Whatever happened to you?"

Craven explained that she had injured her Achilles tendon in her hotel in Mombasa and had been rushed to the hospital for an emergency operation. In preparation for her surgery, she had been given a hospital gown to wear. The gown was exactly as Gray had drawn it after seeing Craven's ghost appear that night a week before—it was a rough, square-cut garment with a ragged neckline.

SOURCE: Inglis, Kim, and Tony Whitehorn (eds.). *Ghosts and Hauntings* (Quest for the Unknown series) (Pleasantville, NY: Reader's Digest, 1993).

CLASS: *Ghost of the Present*
TYPE: *Crisis Apparition*
VARIANT: *Phantom Hitchhiker*

DESCRIPTIVE INCIDENT
DATE: *May 20, 1981*
LOCATION: *Palavas-des-Flots, France*
WITNESSES: *Thierry and Florence, Lionel and Francoise*

Just before midnight, two couples were returning from a day at the beach in their two-door Renault when the driver spotted a woman standing by the roadside. Even though their car was already quite full, the driver decided to stop and pick her up as there would be no public transportation at that hour of the night. The front passenger got out to let the woman in and she settled in snugly between the two women, aged seventeen and twenty, in the rear. The driver told the woman, who was wearing a white mackintosh and headscarf, that they were headed for Montpellier but she said nothing, just nodded her head.

The car continued on its way as music played on the cassette player. Then, just as they were approaching a sharp curve, the woman cried out: "Look out for the turn! You are risking your life!" The driver slowed the car and safely turned the bend, when suddenly he heard the cries of their companions in the backseat. The woman had disappeared.

Shaken, the two couples searched the car, even though there was no way for the woman to have left it. When they arrived at the Montpellier police station in a near panic, Inspector Lopez explained that he was in no mood for a prank. But the witnesses insisted on filing a report. "Their panic wasn't put on and we soon realized they were genuine," said Lopez, finally convinced of their sincerity. "It worried us." A subsequent investigation of the scene of the incident revealed nothing.

One wonders if the apparition did not, in fact, save the two couples from having an accident.

SOURCE: Michael Goss, *The Evidence for Phantom Hitchhikers* (Wellingborough: Aquarian Press, 1984); B Dupi, "La Dame Blanche où quand l'auto-stoppeuse se volatilise," *Lumière dans la Nuit*, March–April, 1982.

GHOSTS OF THE PRESENT

NONCRISIS APPARITIONS

CLASS: *Ghost of the Present*
TYPE: *Noncrisis Apparition*
VARIANT: *Double*

DESCRIPTIVE INCIDENT
DATE: *1845*
LOCATION: *Neuwelcke, Latvia*
WITNESSES: *Antoinette Wrangel and many other students*

Emilie Sagée was thirty-two years old when she left Dijon, France, for Latvia. She was a good and conscientious teacher, though her uncanny ability to be seen by several people simultaneously in more than one place frightened some of the pupils and puzzled the staff.

On one occasion, watched by her thirteen pupils, Sagée turned to the blackboard to illustrate the point she was making. To their amazement, they saw a *second* Sagée appear beside the first, copying her movements precisely. The second teacher was an exact duplicate in every way except that the *real* teacher was holding a piece of chalk, her look-alike empty-handed. The girls were less astonished than they might have been, for soon after the arrival of their new French teacher, stories began to be whispered among the pupils. One said that the young Antoinette Wrangel had fainted one evening while being helped by Sagée to do up her dress—for in the mirror she had seen two Sagées attending to her.

The culminating incident occurred when the entire school—forty-two in all—were assembled in one room, working at their embroidery. Everyone could see Sagée outside in the garden, picking flowers. Suddenly, the teacher watching over them had to leave, but a moment later her place in the armchair was taken by Sagée, though the children could still see the "real" Sagée in the garden. When two girls boldly approached the seated figure and tried to touch her, they found they could pass their hands through the apparition, but felt some resistance like soft material.

Such incidents continued for a year and a half, though only from time to time. They seemed mostly to happen when Sagée was very earnest or eager in what she was doing. It was observed that the more distinct and material to the sight her double was, the more stiff and languid was the real Sagée. She herself knew what was happening, not because she felt any different herself, but because she saw others exchanging looks.

Eventually, word got to the parents, and some of them began taking their children away. When their number dropped to twelve, the director had no choice but to ask Sagée to leave. Though detailed and persuasive, the Sagée claim rests on a single source, one of the pupils, the sister of a well-known spiritualist writer, from whom it was obtained by another well-known spiritualist writer.

SOURCE: Robert Dale Owen, *Footfalls on the Boundary of Another World* (London: Trübner & Co., 1860).

CLASS: *Ghost of the Living*
TYPE: *Noncrisis Apparition*
VARIANT: *Living Other*

DESCRIPTIVE INCIDENT
DATE: *October 3, 1863*
LOCATION: *Atlantic Ocean*
WITNESS: *S. R. Wilmot and Mr. Tait*

Wilmot was on the steamer *City of Limerick*, sailing from Liverpool to New York; his wife and children were back home in Watertown, Connecticut. During the small hours of the morning Wilmot dreamed that he saw his wife in her nightdress approaching the door of his stateroom. At the door she seemed to realize that he was not the only one in the stateroom and hesitated before advancing to his side. But she then stooped down, kissed him, and after caressing him briefly, quietly departed. In the morning, Wilmot learned that the person in the berth above his had been awake and had seen a woman enter, kiss him, and depart, just as Wilmot had experienced. Mr. Tait, the fellow-passenger, made the jocular remark "You're a pretty fellow to have a lady come and visit you in this way."

When Wilmot arrived in Watertown, the first thing his wife asked was whether he had received a visit from her the week before. Wilmot, surprised at her question, reminded her that he had been at sea a thousand miles away at the time. His wife then explained that because another ship had recently run aground, she had been worried about him. On the night of October 3, she had lain awake and it seemed to her that at about four in the morning she had gone out to visit him.

She remembered crossing a stormy sea, coming to a steamship, descending into the cabin and passing through the stern, until she came to his stateroom. (In fact, his wife described the ship perfectly to him, though she had never been aboard it.) She then noticed that there was a man in the slightly recessed upper berth looking at her and was momentarily afraid. But she then bent down, kissed and embraced her husband, and went away.

In all, three people were aware of this "ghost," Mr. Wilmot who thought he was dreaming, the gentleman in the upper berth who was awake, and the ghost herself, Mrs. Wilmot.

SOURCE: Hornell Hart, "Six Theories About Apparitions," *Proceedings of the Society for Psychical Research*, Vol. 50, Part 185, May 1956.

CLASS: *Ghost of the Living*
TYPE: *Noncrisis Apparition*
VARIANT: *Living Other*

DESCRIPTIVE INCIDENT
DATE: *January 1886*
LOCATION: *Botley, Hants, England*
WITNESS: *Mrs. Bedford*

On a Saturday afternoon in early January, Mrs. Murray Gladstone had gone to visit an old couple, the Bedfords, who lived in a cottage just a half mile away. Mrs. Bedford was ill in bed, so Gladstone went upstairs to see her. As she sat there talking to Mrs. Bedford for a few minutes, the thought struck her that the light coming in through the window was very bright and, being directly across the foot of the bed, struck the invalid right in the eyes. She resolved to make a curtain for Mrs. Bedford, but told no one about it.

Gladstone returned to the Bedford residence on Monday, but this time she only saw Mr. Bedford downstairs. "My wife has seen you yesterday [Sunday] morning," he said to Gladstone, following a greeting. "She turned her head towards the side of the bed and said: 'Is that her?' I did not speak, as I thought she was dreaming. 'Yes,' she went on, 'it is Mrs. Gladstone, and she is holding up a curtain with both her hands, but she says it is not long enough. Then she smiled and disappeared.'"

Gladstone then told Mr. Bedford that that is exactly what she had done at her own home on Sunday while dressing. She had gone to the cupboard and had taken out a piece of serge, which she thought would fit Mrs. Bedford's window. She then held it up to her own window with both hands and said to herself: "This is not long enough."

Prior to the Saturday visit, Gladstone had only been to the Bedford home once, a year before. Both times she had worn her "walking dress." But when Mrs. Bedford had *seen* her on Sunday, she was not wearing her bonnet, which was probably the case, noted Gladstone, as this must have occurred before nine in the morning. Subsequently, Mrs. Bedford described Gladstone as having been dressed in white on that Sunday *visit*. "What did I have on my head?" Gladstone asked her. "Something like this," said Mrs. Bedford, holding up an odd-shaped, woolen cap that Gladstone had given her. "It was the facsimile of the one which I must have had on at the time," Gladstone told the investigator.

SOURCE: Edmund Gurney, Frederic W. H. Myers, and Frank Podmore, *Phantasms of the Living,* Vol. II (London: The Society for Psychical Research, 1886).

CLASS: *Ghost of the Living*	**DESCRIPTIVE INCIDENT**
TYPE: *Noncrisis Apparition*	DATE: *January 22, 1901*
VARIANT: *Doppelganger*	LOCATION: *France*
	WITNESS: *Boru*

oru, an eighteen-year-old student, was working late one night preparing for a literature exam. Needing to check a reference, he got up from his worktable and walked into the next room to look for the book he needed. When he found it, he started to return with it to the other room. In the doorway, while holding the book in one hand and the doorknob with the other, Boru suddenly saw himself sitting back at the table, engaged in writing the very words he was at that moment forming in his mind.

He had no idea how long he stood there, but every detail of the scene was clear to him—the lamp, the bookshelf, his notebooks, and ink bottle. But what he found most curious was that he was totally aware, both of standing in front of the door, feeling in his hand the cold metal of the doorknob he was holding, yet at the same time of sitting on his chair and pressing his hand on his pen to write.

Extraordinarily, not only could he see the "other" Boru sitting at the table, but he could see and read the words he was writing. Yet the conscious Boru was standing six to ten feet away, at a distance where he would not have been able to read, by any normal means, what was being written on the table.

A moment later he walked over to the table, and as he moved to sit in his chair the phantom Boru vanished. As he himself expressed it, "Perhaps Boru 1 and Boru 2 became reunited in a single being."

Boru was described as intelligent and in no way neurotic. Nothing like it happened to him before or has since, as far as we know. The intense concentration of his study seems to have been the operative factor; dominated by the preoccupation of finding the reference he needed, his conscious mind was perhaps already anticipating what he would write in his notes. Somehow this provoked the apparent separation, but also the dual consciousness of Boru 1, engaged in obtaining the information he needed, and Boru 2, engaged in transcribing that information to his notes.

It may be relevant, or mere coincidence, that the question he was then working on involved a comparison between two characters from two separate plays by Corneille. Could the idea of these two characters have somehow triggered Boru's own separation into two? It seems far-fetched, but there is no easier explanation.

SOURCE: Gabriel Delanne, *Apparitions des vivants* (Paris: Leymarie, 1909), p. 388.

CLASS: *Ghost of the Present*	**DESCRIPTIVE INCIDENT**
TYPE: *Noncrisis Apparition*	DATE: *1975*
VARIANT: *Doppelganger*	LOCATION: *Roebourne, Western Australia*
	WITNESS: *"George"*

In 1975, "George" was appointed Senior Officer of Roebourne Gaol, or prison, and, since housing was at a premium, took up temporary residence in what had been the single men's quarters in the old part of the building. One night, George woke up for no apparent reason and got out of bed. As he walked out into the passage that led from the bedroom to the living room, he saw the figure of a man standing under the archway that separated the two rooms. Then, just as George said "What the hell are you doing here?" the figure slowly faded out and disappeared.

Some time later, George had a similar experience. He had the night off and was sitting in the armchair next to the fireplace, reading a book and smoking his pipe. His wife had gone to bed early. After dozing off for a while, George came to and noticed that his book had fallen to the floor and the fire was almost out. He then got up to go to the bathroom.

When he returned and reached the doorway, he was "flabbergasted" to find "this man" sitting in his chair, smoking a pipe! "I was positive he was a real live person," George told the interviewer. "I mean to have the cheek to come into my house as if it belonged to him. I just blurted out something like 'who do you think you are—in my chair?' " But just as George spoke, the figure began to fade out.

"It was an incredible experience," said George, in conclusion. "Believe me I've thought about it many times, seeking an answer. *Sometimes I wonder if it was me in the chair*. If my spirit had left my body for an instant, but I can't accept that . . ."

SOURCE: Miriam Howard Wright, *Eyewitness: Australian Ghosts*, (Western Australia: Artlook, 1980).

CLASS: *Ghost of the Living*	**DESCRIPTIVE INCIDENT**
TYPE: *Noncrisis Apparition*	**DATE:** *1990*
VARIANT: *Living Other*	**LOCATION:** *Marin County, California*
	WITNESSES: *"Jean," "Bill," and their two boys*

Just a couple of months after moving from New York to California, Jean and Bill, both in the stock and securities business, and their two boys, aged two and four, began to catch glimpses of an apparition of a little girl of about six years old roaming around their eighty-year-old house.

The little girl acted as if she wanted to play and often followed Jean around the house, even into the car sometimes as Jean prepared to go shopping. But just as Jean was driving away from the house, the apparition would invariably vanish. Once, according to Jean, the little girl appeared in the living room and crawled up into her lap while she was reading. Jean reported being able to feel the weight of the little girl in her lap.

Some time later, Jean found some old photos while fixing up the house. She learned that the couple in the photographs were the people who had built the house. In these pictures were their children, two little girls, one about four, the other about six, with ringlet-style curls, wearing dark dresses with white trim. Jean identified the older of the two girls as their ghostly visitor. When Jean finally tracked down the original family's relatives, she learned that their "ghost" was still alive. The girl was now an ill woman in her nineties who lived in a house right up the street!

Following up on this remarkable coincidence, Jean went to visit the woman, who as it turned out was bedridden. The woman's nurse told Jean that "Mary" frequently floated in and out of consciousness and often spoke of having dreams in which she would revisit her childhood home, which was now Jean's house, and play with the "nice lady now living there."

Loyd Auerbach, who investigated this case, believes Mary was projecting herself into Jean's house. But why was Mary appearing as a little girl? "Mary was visiting the house where she grew up," explains Auerbach, "and remembering a time when she was a little girl. This was her own image of herself at the time of the projections, and therefore was what Jean and the others picked up."

When Jean went to visit Mary, Mary seemed to recognize Jean, though she did not seem to make the connection with the person in her dreams. Some time later when the little girl again appeared in Jean's house, Jean told her that she should stop these visits and concern herself with getting over her illness. The ghostly little girl never returned.

SOURCE: Loyd Auerbach, "An Apparition of the Living," *Fate*, February 1992.

GHOSTS OF THE FUTURE

HARBINGERS

CLASS: *Ghost of the Future*	DESCRIPTIVE INCIDENT
TYPE: *Harbinger*	DATE: *July 1955*
VARIANT: *Vardøgr*	LOCATION: *Oslo, Norway*
	WITNESSES: *Unnamed receptionist and Mr. Olsen*

E rkson Gorique had long wished to visit Norway, but until July 1955, had never found the opportunity. Now, though, the chance had come. The New York importer had crossed the Atlantic to purchase Norwegian china and glassware. After landing at Oslo, he went to reserve a room at a large hotel where, to his astonishment, the receptionist greeted Gorique by name, assuring him that there was a room already reserved for him. Who had made the reservation? Why, said the receptionist, he himself had done so, in person, earlier in the year.

That was strange enough, but things got stranger still the following day, when he went to call on a wholesaler. He had never met Mr. Olsen, but his company had been recommended to him. Like the hotel receptionist, Olsen greeted him by name, saying he was delighted to see him again, the more so, because on the occasion of Gorique's previous visit, the American had seemed in a hurry to get away, saying he planned to come over again in the summer to conclude their business. Gorique's skepticism was confounded when Olsen was able to correctly recall the addresses of his office and warehouse in New York.

When Gorique made it clear that he had never previously set foot in Norway, Olsen introduced him to a university professor, who speculated that his visitor had been preceded by his astral self, known in Norway as the *vardøgr,* literally the "before-goer." The vardøgr is a traditional element of Norwegian folklore. Perhaps the vast distances and extreme weather conditions of the country, which make travel so dangerous, have contributed to this precaution, whereby a traveler unconsciously projects ahead of himself his own replica as a kind of herald, to announce that he is on his way.

SOURCE: Editorial item, "Astral Advance Agent," *Fate*, May 1956, p. 62.

CLASS: *Ghost of the Future*
TYPE: *Harbinger*
VARIANT: *Living Others*

DESCRIPTIVE INCIDENT
DATE: *July 1978*
LOCATION: *Bridgewater, Nova Scotia, Canada*
WITNESSES: *Les Mulhall and Ria*

During Schooner Week in Nova Scotia, Lois and Les Mulhall had numerous friends and family—including their son Peter and his wife Cheryl—staying over at their big old remodeled farmhouse in Bridgewater. One quiet night in the middle of the week, exhausted from partying, they all went to bed early.

Sometime after everyone had fallen asleep, Lois heard the door of their bedroom slam shut, which it could not do on its own as it always snagged in the shag carpet, even on a windy night, which it wasn't. She heard the doorknob rattle as well as someone talking to her. Too sleepy to check on it herself, she awoke Les, who got up to investigate. As she fell back asleep she heard her husband say: "You won't believe what happened to me."

The next morning as everyone gathered for breakfast, their friend Ria blurted out: "You won't believe what happened to me last night." Les then echoed the same statement and told his story. When he had opened their bedroom door, he had seen a woman coming toward him. She was tall and slender and wore a white nightgown with a tie around the waist. The woman had one arm raised, as if touching her hair; the other hung down by her side. Les thought it was Cheryl sleepwalking. He decided to lead her back to her room on the third floor but when he reached out to turn her around, he walked right through her.

Ria then told her story. She awoke when the door of the bedroom next to hers, where Peter and Cheryl were staying, slammed shut. When she looked up she saw a tall young man, whom she thought was Peter, standing inside the doorway. But no matter how she shifted in bed, only half of him appeared to be standing in the doorway—and the door itself was closed.

"Nine days later," wrote Lois Mulhall, "Peter and Cheryl were killed in a small aircraft accident on their way back to Chatham Airforce Base, where Peter was stationed."

SOURCE: John Robert Colombo, *Extraordinary Experiences* (Toronto: Hounslow Press, 1990).

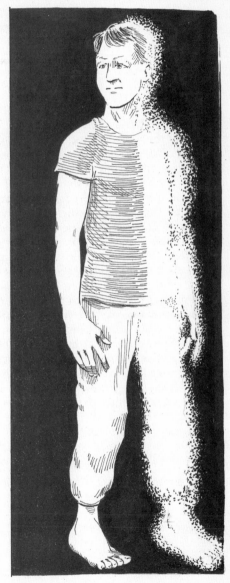

CLASS: *Ghost of the Future*	**DESCRIPTIVE INCIDENT**
TYPE: *Harbinger*	**DATE:** *December 8, 1983*
VARIANT: *Banshee*	**LOCATION:** *Dublin, Ireland*
	WITNESS: *Anne Hill*

It was not Anne Hill's first experience with the banshee. She had heard it when her father's brother had died. And on a Thursday in 1983 she heard the "terrible screaming" again. "It was just like someone was outside the window," recalled Hill. So she ran to the window in the hopes of seeing something, but she couldn't see anything even though the screaming kept getting louder and louder at the window. Since the "piercing scream" was so catlike, Hill went to check on her two cats who, as it turns out, were fast asleep and could obviously hear nothing of this. The screaming then went away, then got louder, and went away—four times altogether, until it faded out for good.

Hill ran upstairs to ask her mother if she had heard anything. She had not. Neither had her sister who was also in the house. "Well," Hill said, "it must be the banshee."

Then the next day when Hill was coming home from work, she saw her mother running down the road and asked if anything was wrong. Her mother replied: "Oh, your Aunt Jane died last night."

Hill did not see the banshee and sightings of this strictly Irish "death messenger" are actually quite rare. While the banshee's appearance in these accounts varies considerably, once unreliable literary records are discarded a fairly consistent description emerges. The banshee is invariably female and, more often than not, old and small. Her hair is generally long and white, and in some parts of Ireland she is seen combing her hair. She is usually wearing a long cloak that is often white, but sometimes red or black.

The banshee usually manifests around a house, oftentimes in a window, and almost always *before* a death takes place.

SOURCE: Patricia Lysaght, *The Banshee: The Irish Death Messenger* (Boulder, Colorado: Robert Rinehart, 1986).

CLASS: *Ghost of the Future*
TYPE: *Harbinger*
VARIANT: *Grim Reaper without Scythe*

DESCRIPTIVE INCIDENT
DATE: *Mid-1990s*
LOCATION: *Erie, Pennsylvania*
WITNESSES: *Unnamed nurses*

The witness had worked as a registered nurse for nearly twenty years by the time this particular encounter occurred. She was then employed at a long-term care facility in Erie, Pennsylvania.

On this particular night a resident, who had no family or friends, lay dying. He was the only person in the room; the other bed was empty. The nurse was talking softly with an LPN (licensed practical nurse) outside his room, when suddenly they both stopped speaking, stunned at what they were seeing. Facing the dying man was a "black-robed figure, with hood, standing at the foot of the resident's bed," the nurse wrote in reporting the incident to Mark Chorvinsky. "He made no move toward the resident but seemed content to stand, waiting."

"Did you see that?" the nurse asked the LPN. She had, but another nurse who had stood there with them had not. If the resident ever saw anything, he never said so. In any case, he died the following night.

This nurse claims to have seen similar reaperlike figures in hospitals and nursing homes on several occasions. Usually the dark, robed figure is standing near the nurse's station or in the hall. On rare occasions, she says, the figure is white. Never has she heard the figure speak, but invariably someone dies within a few days of its appearance.

This is one of many grim reaper encounters witnessed by nurses and collected for a study of the subject by Chorvinsky.

SOURCE: Mark Chorvinsky, "Encounters with the Grim Reaper," *Strange Magazine*, No. 18, Summer 1997.

GHOSTS OF THE FUTURE

TIME SLIPS

CLASS: *Ghost of the Future*
TYPE: *Time Slip*
VARIANT: *Airbase*

DESCRIPTIVE INCIDENT
DATE: *1935*
LOCATION: *Drem, Scotland*
WITNESS: *Sir Victor Goddard*

One day Sir Victor Goddard, a wing commander of the Royal Air Force, was flying over Scotland when he got caught in the buildup of a giant thunderstorm. To avoid getting torn apart, he cut back the power on his Hawker Hart biplane fighter and started coming down through the clouds. He knew he was near Edinburgh, with its abandoned airfield at Drem.

As he broke through the cloud deck, a shaft of sunlight illuminated the countryside below. But instead of an abandoned airfield Goddard found himself approaching an airfield bustling with activity. At a height of only thirty feet, according to the report he later filed with the Royal Air Force, he could see open hangar doors, living quarters, vehicles, a handful of airplanes, and people milling about. But there was something *wrong*. The airplanes, including a monoplane he was unfamiliar with, were all painted yellow instead of the standard silver and the mechanics' uniforms were blue instead of brown.

Goddard then made another roaring pass at the field, which oddly enough was completely ignored by the airmen below, and recognized all the landmarks of the Drem airfield which he had just visited the previous day. Its runways had then been broken, its buildings collapsed, and the field deserted. As his airplane cleared the fourth of the newly covered buildings, Goddard was plunged again in the rainstorm and he returned to Turnhouse, where he had begun his trip.

Four years later on the eve of World War II, Drem reopened as a training field with its aircraft painted yellow. The blue overalls for mechanics had been introduced in 1938. And monoplanes like the Miles Magister Goddard had seen were now in service for the first time.

SOURCE: Victor Goddard, *Flight Towards Reality* (London: Turnstone, 1975).

CLASS: *Ghost of the Future*
TYPE: *Time Slip*
VARIANT: *Building*

DESCRIPTIVE INCIDENT
DATE: *Summer 1981*
LOCATION: *Edmonton, Canada*
WITNESS: *"Amy Meredith"*

During her first visit to Edmonton on a business trip, "Amy Meredith" was traveling on a freeway in a taxi when she saw a building at a crossroads, which she assumed must be the legislative building. "It was a very large, impressive-looking building made of reddish brown bricks" that sat on a grassy knoll overlooking a wide blue river.

"It was like a tableau," she recalled. As the taxi rounded a bend, Meredith continued looking at the sight over her left shoulder. She was surprised that Edmonton should have anything as "lovely" as this building, which she observed for about two minutes. The incident had a "powerful effect" on her, making her feel strangely excited and elated.

When Meredith returned to Edmonton for a vacation with her fourteen-year-old son in 1985, she was eager to visit the West Edmonton Mall and, of course, the legislative building that had so impressed her four years earlier. But when she saw the real legislative building, she was very disappointed and surprised. Where could "my" building be, she wondered?

Meredith later contacted the Tourist Board of Edmonton, but these people had no knowledge of any such building. Nevertheless they sent her many brochures, maps, and pictures of Edmonton, in the hopes she could identify the building, but it was to no avail.

Meredith, who claims to be "psychically sensitive," especially when traveling, is certain that she did not glimpse a scene from Edmonton's past. But if it was a scene from another city's past, why would it show up here, she wondered? Could it have been from another dimension, she speculated. Could it have been a scene from Edmonton's own *future?*

SOURCE: Andrew Mac Kenzie, *Adventures in Time* (London: Athlone, 1997).

AFTERWORD

HALLUCINATION HYPOTHESIS

Each and every one of these fifty cases happened to someone: each is evidence of a Ghost Experience. The fact that people have been reporting such experiences throughout the history of mankind is evidence that ghosts clearly exist, if only as a recurring concept in popular belief. But are they more than that? Is the Ghost Experience an encounter with an otherworldly entity—or merely an artifact of the human imagination?

Clearly, ghosts don't exist in the everyday sense of the word. They pass through locked doors, they make themselves visible to some people and not to others, they glide rather than walk, they are self-illuminating so they can be seen in the dark, they appear and then vanish abruptly and mysteriously. These are not flesh-and-blood creatures. There is nothing else in our experience of the universe which does all these things. We have no conceptual framework into which we can fit them, so we have had to create a special category for them. A ghost is a ghost is a ghost.

But that's not good enough for scientists. They have a requirement to fit all phenomena, all events, all experiences, into the framework which constitutes our knowledge of the universe. A place must be found, somewhere in that framework, for ghosts. So, to scientists, a ghost is a hallucination, by which they mean an illusion, "the apparent perception of an external object or sense-datum when no such object or stimulus is present," as the *Shorter Oxford Dictionary* defines it.

Up to a point, the scientists are correct. Strictly speaking, there is no evidence for an object which corresponds to ghosts. Along with alien entities, visions of saints and other otherworldly beings, there is no evidence that ghosts possess any existence *as objects* in the commonly accepted sense of the word. But we have seen that there is abundant evidence that ghosts do present a *stimulus*: The witness is stimulated by something into the very real experience of supposing that he or she is seeing a ghost.

And that stimulus cannot be simply an internal artifact, something created by and within the mind of the witness. Haunting cases show it to be otherwise. Take the case of Miss J. A. A., a young Englishwoman who went to stay with her cousins in the country, and was visited in the night by the ghost of a small girl. When she told everyone of her experience, the family pretended to dismiss it as a nightmare, until one of the cousins finally admitted that the little girl had been seen by three other members of the family, on three separate occasions. Since Miss J. A. A. had known nothing of this, something must have caused her to see the ghost of the girl. The same is true of such haunters as Cheltenham's Imogen Swinhoe (see page 66), seen independently by so many witnesses.

When the eminent English researcher Frank Podmore considered such cases, he concluded they could be accounted for by *telepathic hallucination*: that is, the ghost originates within the mind of some individual or other, and is subsequently communicated to other minds by telepathy. But this is explaining one mystery by another. Even if we grant that telepathy exists—which of course scientists are not about to do—we are left with the fact that something is transmitted from the originating individual to the subsequent witnesses. And that something is not nothing, it is a message, an item of information technology of a kind which is as yet unrecognized. That message is the stimulus which is supposed to be lacking when a person hallucinates. In other words, ghosts are not simply hallucinations.

The same has to be true of crisis apparitions. Hallucinations they may be, but they are shared hallucinations. When the apparent is in a crisis situation, how is this information shared with the witness? The same kind of paranormal data-transfer that Podmore proposed is in operation. And once again, that is rather more than what the scientists mean by hallucination, for they would have it that there is nothing, nothing at all, outside the mind of the perceiving witness.

Even if we make a further concession, and suppose that the apparent has nothing to do with the crisis apparition, that it is the witness himself who is somehow aware of it, and stages the whole episode within his own mind, let's say—even then, the implication is that the mind of the witness has received signals of some kind, signals which bring him the information with which he creates his staged vision. This is information he certainly did not already possess for how could he know that, say, his aunt Jane was involved in a railway accident (as he later learns to be the case), or that she was wearing a red scarf and a white coat at the time (as also turns out to be the case)? That signal—the message telling him about the accident—is just as much a stimulus, just as much an item of paranormal information technology, just as "real," as if aunt Jane sent her ghost to call on him.

All this may seem hair-splitting logic-chopping to the person who is convinced he or she has a ghost experience. But it is a necessary process if we are to do what the scientists want us to do, and find a place for the ghost in our picture of the universe.

SOUND REASONS

Science, of course, is still far more interested in explaining away ghosts than in explaining what they are. Its latest sound reason for ghosts emerged by chance when an expert in computer-assisted learning experienced a haunting in the laboratory of a medical manufacturing company in the English Midlands. Vic Tandy had been told that the building he was working in was haunted, but he dismissed the idea as a joke. Then late one night while working alone he began to feel as if someone was in the room with him. And though he was sweating, Tandy felt strangely cold and depressed. A "figure" then emerged slowly to his left. "It was indistinct and on the periphery of my vision," Tandy recalled in an interview with science journalist Robert Matthews, "but it moved just as I would expect a person to. It was gray, and made no sound. The hair was standing up on the back of my neck—I was terrified." When Tandy finally looked at the apparition straight on, however, it vanished. Thinking he was "cracking up," Tandy went home.

But Tandy—and reason—returned in the morning. A fencing enthusiast, he had left the blade of one of his foils in a clamp while going off in search of oil. When he returned, he noticed that the free end of the blade was vibrating frantically. Trained as an engineer, Tandy realized that the blade must be receiving energy from a very low frequency sound, one that was too low to be heard. The culprit turned out to be a new, improperly-mounted extraction fan that caused the air in the room to vibrate at about nineteen cycles per second. This vibration produced a "standing wave" in the laboratory that, as it turned out, reached a peak intensity right next to Tandy's desk. When the fan's setting was fixed, the "haunting" ceased. That all happened twenty years ago.

Now at Coventry University, Tandy has discovered the significance of this rate of vibration. Working with Tony Lawrence of the university's school of health, Tandy found that "infra-sound" around this frequency was linked to symptoms of hyperventilation—breathlessness, shivering, and feelings of fear—which are similar to panic attacks and would also explain the feelings of dread Tandy reported. But even more to the point, the eye, as it happens, has a resonant frequency around 18–20 Hz. "Mechanical vibration of any kind at that frequency will make the eyeball resonate accordingly," Lawrence explains. "This kind of vibration would create visual disturbances or a smearing of vision."

Tandy has since come across two more hauntings that could be traced to similar low-frequency sound disturbances. One occurred in the hallway of a building that housed a wind tunnel. But since most homes where apparitions occur lack large extraction fans and wind tunnels, Tandy suggests that all you would need to create a standing wave and concoct a ghost is a long windy corridor. It would be like blowing over the neck of a bottle, he notes.

Still, Tandy and Lawrence need not be reminded of the limited explanatory power of their standing wave theory. "If someone says they saw a full blown vision of a man wearing a tweed jacket, with a black Labrador dog that barked when the man said 'Down Boy!' " notes Lawrence, "then the standing wave theory doesn't even come close to an explanation." Indeed.

MEMORY TRACES AND PSI-SUBSTANCE

Hallucinations and standing waves are not, of course, the only theories offered to explain ghosts. As far as haunters are concerned, there have been suggestions that something like a "memory trace" has been left behind, somewhat like the tape recording of a voice, and this is being picked up by the various witnesses. While admittedly the idea is ingenious, there is no evidence that any such thing as a "memory trace" exists, and no indication as to what kind of process would enable it to be detected by the witness, especially since only certain kinds of people seem to be able to detect it. Or should we think of it as being like a smell to which some people are acutely sensitive while others do not even notice it?

Perhaps some such thinking lies behind the suggestion that there may exist some kind of substance which is the "building material" used to construct ghosts, phantom animals, and other things which exist on the frontier between fact and fantasy. In a lecture given to the London Society for Psychical Research in 1937, C. A. Mace was "of the opinion that we can, with a good scientific conscience, postulate the existence of a medium which records impressions of patterns of events, and which later or elsewhere may produce a corresponding pattern." Another member of this Society, the philosopher H. H. Price, agreed, and proposed a kind of "psi-substance" which would, for a while at least, continue to exist even when the individual's physical body was dead. Clearly, this would account for both hauntings and revenants, and by extension, for crisis apparitions also.

But what is this psi-substance? Is it really anything more than a more neutral, more "scientific" label for the *astral body*—that invisible part of us which supposedly, according to occult tradition, each of us possesses together with our physical body? Our astral body, it is held, detaches itself from our physical body during out-of-the-body experiences. It may be that part of us which survives while our physical body crumbles into dust. If so, it just could be the stuff that ghosts are made of. Moreover, the concept of an astral, or nonphysical "second body" explains how it is that there are phantoms of the living as well as ghosts of the dead. If this theory is correct—and we need this theory, or something like it, to explain the many categories of ghost—each and every one of us possesses a second body of this sort.

Having said that, however, we must account for the fact that most of us pass our lives—and perhaps our deaths also—without ever separating our astral body from our physical one. Just as only a minority of people have out-of-body experiences, so only a few people manifest as ghosts, whether during their lifetimes or subsequently. Whether these people are somehow specially constituted so that it comes more easily to them than to others, or whether particular conditions are required for this to happen, is anybody's guess. Perhaps both are true. The "you-are-our-ghost" type of case, in which a living person subsequently recognizes a ghost as actually being a living person, suggests that there are some people whose second body detaches itself spontaneously, though that does not explain why it always travels to the same destination and familiarizes itself with someone else's home (see page 118).

But in this day and age astral bodies are out of fashion and "psi-substance" is only one of the concepts that researchers have suggested to replace them. Some theosophists suppose that ghosts may be "thought-forms." Meanwhile the skeptical scientist will protest that this is all nonsense, that there isn't a scrap of evidence for psi-stuff, memory traces, thought-forms, or any other of these explanations. That may well be so, but haunting ghosts *are* the evidence, the experience that underlies all the speculation.

CLOSE ASSOCIATIONS

One way of separating the diversity of ghosts is by considering whether they relate to people or places. Haunting ghosts seem, almost always, linked to one particular place; Imogen Swinhoe of Cheltenham (see page 66), for example, isn't seen anywhere else. Haunters don't travel. And it doesn't seem to matter to haunters who sees them—in fact, they invite the intriguing question, do haunters haunt even when there's no one around to see them do it? Such a question could, in principle, be resolved by mounting a closed-circuit TV camera to monitor the haunting site, and this has, of course, been attempted, but hitherto without conclusive success. As advanced technology gets to be less expensive and more sophisticated, however, this could yet be the way to scientific evidence, uncontaminated by human susceptibilities.

By contrast to the place-related haunters, there are ghosts who seem definitely to target a particular person among the living, who may see them in various places—or even in more than one place at the same time. Consider this case: On October 18, 1940, a man was walking through the streets of Zurich on his way back to his office, when he was surprised to see his father who was away and not expected back anytime soon. So the man quickened his steps and called out "Hello, father!" whereupon the figure suddenly disappeared. The man then continued on to his office, wondering if he had been dreaming. As soon as he returned to his desk he received a call from a relative who told him that his father had died of a stroke during the night. The man then called his sister to give her the bad news. She at once replied that she also had seen their father in the Bahnhoffstrasse at exactly the same time. And he too had vanished suddenly.

If the ghost were what it purports to be, the spirit of the dead man, we would have to suppose that it went first to one street, to be seen by the brother, then hurried to another street, in order to be seen by the sister. But as soon as we start speculating in such terms, we realize how absurd it is to assume that ghosts are restricted in the way we humans are. For all we know, ghosts may be able to manifest in half a dozen places at once. But of one thing there is no doubt: that ghost targeted the son and daughter, and no one else. Unlike a haunter, who doesn't seem to care who sees it, many crisis apparitions are choosy about who sees them.

Yet, having said that, there are cases which show that things aren't always quite so simple and straightforward. Consider this revealing crisis apparition case. The date is August 1864; the place is Barbados. May Clerke is reading in the verandah while a native nurse is pushing her little girl in a pram. When Clerke gets up to go into the house, the nurse asks who the gentleman was who had just been talking to her. Clerke replies that no one has been speaking to her. The nurse insists there was, that the gentleman was very pale and very tall. Clerke becomes cross with the nurse when she says that Clerke, in never answering the man, had been very rude. A few days later Clerke learns that her brother had died in Tobago just at the time of the apparition. "Now, the curious part is this," said Clerke, "that I did not see him, but she—a stranger to him—did; and she said that he seemed very anxious for me to notice him."

This is curious, indeed, but quite explainable if we speculate that for some reason the brother was unable to get through to his sister, so chose an alternative "channel." But just think what this implies: that the brother was actually there in some sense, in the Barbados garden, trying to get his sister's attention, but failing to do so, looked around for someone who would do instead. It wasn't only a ghostlike figure, it was also a conscious mind, equipped with its human senses, able to see the nurse and make himself visible to her when he had failed with his sister.

The great majority of revenants also seem to be directed at a selected individual, who recognizes them and may even communicate with them. But revenants, too, can appear in more than one place, and show themselves to more than one person. In London in 1957, a brother and his two sisters, living on the same street but in two separate houses, all separately received visitations from their dead mother, according to a case that appeared in the *Archives of General Psychiatry*. The psychologist who examined the witnesses diagnosed it as a *folie à trois*—a shared delusion, a collective hallucination. But that is hardly an explanation. Here again, as in the Zurich case, it is ridiculous to think of the ghost as a kind of nonphysical clone of the apparent, visiting each of her children in turn. Yet at the same time, each child was aware of having an individual experience, directed at himself or herself.

INTERNAL OR EXTERNAL?

So, in the case of haunters and many crisis apparitions, the conclusion seems inescapable: There is no way of ruling out some element external to the witness. Simple hallucination is just not adequate as a complete explanation. The same seems to be true of other kinds of phantasms of the living. In "you-are-our-ghost" cases, for example, the apparent is seen in places where her physical body isn't, so there has to be *something* which acts as the stimulus for the sighting, whether it's psi-substance, or a telepathic message, or something else.

And what about revenants, those ghosts who seem to be returning from the dead? In some cases it is quite easy to believe that the ghost is created by the mind of the witness, as when a recently bereaved widow has momentary sightings of her spouse. A psychologist would account for this as the consequence of wishful thinking, or mere force of habit, and we would find it hard to argue. But if we are forced to admit an agency external to the witness in the cases of haunters and crisis apparitions, we can't rule out the possibility that these revenants, too, are just what they appear to be, the dead returning to comfort or reassure.

Another emotion which might reasonably lead to an imagined sighting is guilt. Shakespeare has Macbeth see the ghost of Banquo, murdered by his orders. And Daniel Defoe tells two stories which, interestingly, point in contrasting directions. His first story is of "a certain man who was brought to the bar of justice on suspicion of murder, which, however, he knew it was not in the power of human knowledge to detect. He pleaded Not guilty, and the court began to be at a loss for a proof, nothing but suspicion and circumstances appearing." But the man himself broke down and confessed, having seen, standing in the witness box "the murder'd person standing as a witness, ready to be examined against him, and ready to shew his throat which was cut by the prisoner." Defoe comments that there was no real apparition, no specter, ghost or appearance. "It was all figur'd out to him by the power of his own guilt, and the agitations of his soul."

We might well agree with him. But another of Defoe's stories from *Secrets of the Invisible World Disclos'd* invites quite a different interpretation. He tells of Lady Osborne who was visited by the apparition of her husband in their country house at the exact moment he died in the West Indies. The dead man reproached her for her extravagant lifestyle and warned her to change her ways. Subsequently, it was learned that the same apparition had appeared a few hours earlier to a servant girl in his London house, taking the elaborate precaution of pretending to be an inquirer who wanted to rent an apartment in the house.

Defoe was basically skeptical. Was it likely, he asks, that when Sir John's mind was occupied with his imminent death, his spirit would stop at the London house and engage in mundane conversation with Mary the maid, then go on to his country house to remonstrate with his wife? Surely it was her guilt, rather than his concern, which inspired the ghost.

But this does not account for Mary's sighting, of a master she had never met, at the time of his death. She did not recognize him for who he was, until later when she described her sighting to Lady Osborne. Doesn't it seem more likely that Sir John's ghost would first go to his London house, expecting to find his wife there, then, after talking with the servant, go on to the other house? Don't we have here a case similar to the Barbados sighting, of a crisis apparition behaving in a quite natural and human-like manner?

Once again, the behavior of Sir John's ghost implies an actual *presence*. The adoption of a pretext of inquiring about the house, the visit first to the London house then to the country home, are just such decisions as a living person might make. They imply that Sir John's ghost was in full possession of his mental faculties, while at the same time enjoying the freedom of movement that only a ghost possesses.

MUTUAL AGREEMENT

It is also possible to think of haunters, and perhaps some other categories of ghosts, as wholly autonomous. The grieving specter haunts the ruined castle without directing its activities at any individual witness, seemingly careless of who sees it, careless indeed of whether it is seen or not. At the other extreme, it is possible to think of revenants as being "all-in-the-mind," fantasies created by the grief or the guilt of the witness.

But with other ghosts—and they are probably the majority—it does not seem possible to go for one or the other of these extreme explanations. Rather, everything points to a kind of cooperation between the one who is seen and the one who sees. The instigation may come from the apparent —the Barbados brother, Sir John Osborne—but it takes some kind of receptiveness on the other's part to bring about a successful manifestation. May Clerke fails to see her brother, but the nurse does, which suggests that the nurse is a better "receiver" than her mistress.

The need for cooperation is particularly striking in the case of ghosts who are seen in a place where they had never been in their lives. Typically, a revenant will materialize in the witness's bedroom, stand at the foot of the bed, and gaze at the witness. But how can it know where to stand, where to look, unless it is actually *there?*

One way of accounting for this is to suppose that it is the witness's mind which, as it were, tells the ghost where to stand, where to look. But this won't do for our Barbados case. The brother leans over his sister's chair in an endeavor to get her attention, but it can't be his sister who tells him where to place himself, because she is totally unaware of his presence. Nor can we think that the information comes from the nurse, because she doesn't know that he is trying to communicate with his sister, and at first takes him for a living person. The most probable explanation is that it is the ghost itself which knows where to position itself, and that leaves us, inescapably, with the conclusion that the ghost is, in some sense, really *there*.

It then remains for the witness to play her part. While Clerke fails, the nurse substitutes for her successfully. We can only wonder how many ghost appearances *fail* because the witness remains unaware of the ghost's presence and there is no one else conveniently around.

FOLKLORE GHOSTS

Although most ghosts are of human beings like ourselves, whether alive or dead, we have seen that there are many categories which appear to relate to beings of other species. To account for the banshee, the Grim Reaper, and others of that ilk, we need an explanation other than the "second body," or "telepathic hallucination," or any theory which is based on human attributes or abilities alone.

Many would exclude these categories of apparition from "true" ghosts, and perhaps they are right to do so. But at the same time, these entities often *act* like ghosts, they manifest in the same mysterious way, they share with ghosts their insubstantial nature but also their ability to stimulate the senses, to make people think they have seen them. To provoke a response from the witness, there has to be *something*.

Folklorists, claiming banshees and their kind for their own, consider them as cultural artifacts, fantasies which have captured the popular imagination and, as the result of centuries of story-telling, have taken on a kind of life of their own. But only as ideas. If a traveler, wandering in a forest at night, mistakes a swinging branch for a scary creature, they would say this is entirely the product of his imagination.

Often, no doubt, that is the case. But not everyone is happy to relegate these entities to all-in-the-mind illusions. A long-held occult tradition holds that such creatures can in fact be *created* by the mind. The noted French traveler in Tibet, Alexandra David-Neel, claimed to have deliberately created a *tulpa* in the form of a Buddhist monk, a being who emanated from her own mind and will, but who then took on a life of his own, and in fact became rather tiresome so that she had to get rid of him—a task which she accomplished only with great difficulty.

All kinds of theories have been proposed for this phenomenon. "Thought-forms" of one kind or another are a favorite label, and Theosophists developed an elaborate system whereby different states of mind and personalities produced corresponding astral counterparts which could be detected by an adept.

It has even been suggested that there exist entities who, while they do not exist on the same physical plane as ourselves, are sufficiently physical that they can interact with us humans. Though often referred to as "demons," they are not necessarily malevolent, though frequently mischievous and even malicious. The eminent Spanish researcher Salvador Freixedo has proposed that these beings are responsible for a number of puzzling phenomena. Their outstanding feature, for the purposes of our inquiry, is their ability to assume any form they like, and to do so in response to human thought. In a classic UFO abduction case in Zimbabwe in 1974, the witness reported: "Another form was beamed straight to the backseat of the car and sat there the entire journey and told me I would see what I wanted to see. If I wanted it to look like a duck, then it would look like a duck; if I wanted it to look like a monster, it would look like a monster."

So, if a person at a critical moment expects to see a harbinger of death, or looks hopefully for a rescuer, one of these demons would pick up his thought and manifest accordingly, taking on the shape of the Grim Reaper, for example. Here again, we have a kind of cooperation. It takes two to make even a folklore ghost. But this time, the partnership is not between the witness and a fellow human being, alive or dead, but with a creature from the borderlands of existence, normally invisible to our eyes, but able to take on a short-lived identity during which it mirrors what we expect, or hope, or fear to see.

It's a fancy theory, but is there really any convincing evidence that such beings exist? Anecdotes abound, and Nicholas Mamontoff tells a fine story of a group of Russian occultists who, under the guidance of a guru, collectively conjured up an *egrigor* simply by the combined force of their collective imaginations. It must be confessed that, so far as evidence goes, the case is weak. On the other hand, such an explanation could account for a vast array of puzzling experiences. Time and time again, sane healthy people are having vivid sightings of otherworldly entities, only to be told by the folklorist or the behavioral scientist that it is simply a product of their imagination. No doubt, these apparitions do indeed have their *origin* in our minds, but if researchers like Freixedo are correct, that is only half the story. To manifest with such convincing force, they must also involve the cooperation of something outside ourselves.

Such a theory could also help us to understand two other puzzling aspects of the ghost phenomenon. Why do so many ghosts commence as balls of light? Could it simply be that this is the "natural" form of these intermediate beings? So, in our mountain rescue case (see page 96), what Frau Schmidt-Falk saw was, first, the "demon" in its undifferentiated form, which then resolved into something more acceptable to human eyes. In most cases, of course, what the witness sees, perhaps, is the apparition in its final form, not its early stages as a light form.

The same theory also accounts for the countless photographs which, when developed, contain inexplicable blobs of light of which the photographer was not aware at the time the picture was taken. Perhaps the camera, uninfluenced by human perception, records what is actually there, which human eyes for some reason cannot detect. Indeed, this would also help us to understand such cases as the Queen's House ghost (see page 82) where nothing was seen by the couple who took the photo, though it is clearly there on the film.

And if it is the case that banshees, harbingers of death, and suchlike have a degree of objective existence, then we can see that they have much in common with ghosts of the living or the dead. Like ghosts, they haunt the borderlands between our everyday reality and the realms of the imagination. It seems reasonable to suppose that the same processes of manifestation on the apparition's part, and of perception on the witness's part, are involved whether we are seeing a "true" ghost, a phantom hitchhiker, a guardian angel, or the Grim Reaper.

WHY AREN'T GHOSTS NAKED?

There is one question about ghosts that initially seems trivial, but which is actually very puzzling and may be essential to an understanding of ghosts. It is the matter of what ghosts wear.

Ghosts generally come wrapped. Naked ghosts, like our case

from Mexico City (see page 42), are quite rare. Yet if ghosts are what they are widely supposed to be, revenants from the next world, this is really rather surprising. We need clothes in this world, either to keep warm or to conform with notions of propriety, but surely in the next world the spirits will abandon the use of clothes with all their inconveniences?

Whichever way we look at the issue, we run into absurdities. Perhaps they *do* wear clothes in the next world, but if so, they surely won't go on wearing the same clothes that they wore on Earth, would they? If there are clothes in the next world, surely they would be very different from ours. As Frank Podmore wondered in 1909, "Ghosts always appear clothed. Have clothes also ethereal counterparts? Again, ghosts commonly appear, not in the clothes which they were wearing at death, but in some others. Are we to suppose the ethereal body going to its wardrobe to clothe its nakedness?"

Either way, naked or trailing gowns of glory, do we suppose that they change back into Earth-style clothes when they return as ghosts, so as not to offend us, and perhaps so as to be recognized? Once again, as soon as we try to understand ghosts in human terms, we run into absurdity.

But the problem remains. The only way out of it is to suppose that in some way a ghost is a projected image, and its clothes bear the same relation to reality as those worn by an actor on TV. But what kind of image can give the illusion of being three-dimensional, can locate itself in a room, adjust itself to the position of the furniture, look the witness in the face, and in every way behave as though it were really *there?*

THE RECOGNITION FACTOR

Do ghosts exist when nobody is looking at them? That is a philosophical question which we have no means of answering. But even if we do not know why ghosts exist, we can adopt as a reasonable working hypothesis that their purpose is to be seen. In which case, it is essential that they should be not only seen, but also *recognized.*

As to *why* ghosts manifest, there may be many reasons. But in some cases, if not all, they seem to have a definite purpose—to convey information, or a warning, or somehow make up for something done or not done during their lifetime. If so, identification of the ghost is all-important.

Early this century, a curious case occurred in Denver, Colorado. A girl named Stella Dean was seen on several occasions in the company of the ghost of a young woman. Investigation revealed that the ghost was that of Hester Holt, who had disappeared from their workplace some time earlier. One night, Stella was found dead, either because she took her own life, or suffered a severe shock. It was presumed, though never proved, that Stella had murdered Hester in a fit of jealousy. What concerns us is the fact that it was crucial that the ghost of Hester should be recognized—she *had* to appear in her own clothes, and looking like her living self, otherwise her identity would never have been revealed and her murderer would have been undetected.

Clearly, recognition is a key factor in many ghost visitations, and it is likely that the need to be identified provides the clue to many puzzling aspects of ghosts, spirits, and other entities. Somehow, those responsible for creating the ghost—and if we are correct in saying that it takes two to make a ghost, this means the witness as well as the apparent—must effect a balance between establishing the *nature* of the ghost (that is, making it obvious to the witness that what he or she is seeing is a ghost) and establishing the identity of the ghost as an individual. In other words, the ghost must be sufficiently ghostlike to be seen to be a ghost, and at the same time sufficiently lifelike that there is no question of its identity.

Which is probably why we do not see many naked ghosts.

GHOST SHIPS AND THINGS

While some of us might be able to conceive of a *person* coming back from the dead, how could some *thing*, like a ship, let's say, (see page 38) rise from its watery grave? Surely there can be no process whereby so inanimate an object can once again sail the seas. But then again maybe there is—if we think of the ship as a haunter. That is, something that left some lingering portion or image of itself behind, sailing out of its own time-frame into the years to come.

Our best agenda for haunters is that for one reason or another—guilt or remorse, unfulfilled promises or duties, the desire for vengeance—they fail to achieve the complete dying process. Whether by choice or by constraint, *something* of them remains whose function is to take care of the unfinished business. But only with difficulty can we imagine a ship having any such emotions.

On the other hand, it is easy to imagine that its *crew* might well have them. So perhaps it is the collective emotion of the ship's company which somehow keeps the vessel afloat in its spectral form. And so with the ghost trains that rattle through deserted stations, and automobile apparitions that haunt dangerous crossroads. During the 1930s, phantom aircraft were seen over Norway, airborne in weather conditions that would have grounded any real aircraft of the day. Were these the planes of flyers who had recklessly tried to fly in such conditions, but failed to make it?

Thinking along these lines raises questions that, at first glance, might seem far afield from the subject at hand. Could UFOs be flying-machines time-traveling from the future, as some have suggested? Our Drem airfield case (see page 132) shows that such a concept is not as outrageous as it seems, but it raises the question we have already asked concerning the Versailles case (see page 26), whether Goddard was flying into the future, or was the future returning to him? Is this precognition or is it time-travel?

It is tempting to dodge the issue by suggesting that such incidents occur outside time altogether, but that can't be the case. What Goddard saw at Drem were airfield staff engaged in activities—that is, performing tasks in a time sequence. They may have been outside Goddard's time-frame, but they were none the less in one of their own. And those airfield staff—were they ghosts? Or was it Goddard himself who was the ghost? Remember that those on the airfield paid no attention to him or his noisy aircraft flying above. Could it have been his own phantom—his double, his projected self—which was traveling forward in time to that airfield which would not exist in that form for years to come?

A MATTER OF TIME

In this work, we have separated ghosts into those from the past, those of the present, and those of the future. Seen from our here-and-now point of view, there certainly do seem to be ghosts from the past—ghosts of our ancestors, ghosts who lived in our house years before we did and who continue to haunt it in the present and perhaps will into the future when we are no longer around. But consider the matter from the ghost's point of view: Are they moving through the years as they did during their lifetime, or are they trapped in an eternal present, which carries them forward from their day to ours, but which is nevertheless still and always the present as far as they are concerned?

Time is a relative thing, of course, and the separation into past, present, and future categories is somewhat artificial. But time does seem to be of the essence: Why do some harbingers appear a week or more in advance, while others do so just a day or less ahead? And if crisis apparitions are by definition "timely," what does this make revenants? Have they missed the train, so to speak? Could ghosts be a byproduct of the warp and weave of time, or is this just an illusion? If the first question that ghosts force us to confront is "What do we mean by real?" the second, surely, is "What do we mean by 'time'?" Perhaps, however, we'll first need to answer the latter before we can ever judge conclusively the former.

We will all know the truth one day, of that we can be fairly certain. It's just a matter of time.

ACKNOWLEDGMENTS

Chris Woodyard unknowingly provided the inspiration for this book through her delightful mail-order catalog of ghost books called Invisible Ink, which no longer exists in print, but is available on the web at *www.invink.com* (or order by phone at 1-800-31-GHOST). She also kindly loaned us some material for cases from Down Under. Many other people helped us in one way or another with this book. Antonio Huneeus provided the South American cases and Isabela Herranz assisted on the Spanish cases. Loren Coleman, Scott Corales, Paul Cropper, Dennis Stacy, Marcello Truzzi, and Dave Walsh also passed on various reports on the subject or otherwise assisted us. And the Mary Evans Picture Library in London contributed some very useful visual reference materials.

We are grateful as well to Loyd Auerbach, Mark Chorvinsky, John Robert Colombo, and Dave Oester for answering specific questions we had about cases in which they had been involved in one way or another. Joanne McMahon, while at the Parapsychology Foundation Library in New York, gave us many good pointers and tried to steer us straight, while Jeff Twine, for his part, dug out materials for us at the library of the American Society for Physical Research, also in New York. Loren Coleman—again—and Michael Grosso kindly commented on one phase or another of our constantly evolving classification scheme, though they should in no way be held responsible for the outcome. And a final tip of the hat goes to veteran investigator Andrew Mackenzie, whose authoritative books we could not have done without.

The subject of ghosts is an ancient one and many people have thought hard about the puzzle they represent—in some cases long before we were even born. We did our best to stand on their shoulders without falling off. Thank you all.

BIBLIOGRAPHY

Adare Viscount. *Experiences in Spiritualism with Mr. D. D. Home*. London: Privately Published, 1869.

Alexander, John. *Ghosts: Washington Revisited*. Atglen PA: Schiffer, 1998.

Anonymous [Annie Moberly and Eleanor Jourdain]. *An Adventure*. London: Macmillan, 1911.

Anonymous, Eleanor Mondale story in column "People in the News," Associated Press, April 14, 1998.

Anonymous, "Ghost of Hemingway stalks Cuban estate," Reuters, April 4, 1998.

Anonymous, "Madrid museum guard says ghost has made him depressed, nervous," Reuters, Feb. 20, 1998.

Anson, Jay. *The Amityville Horror: A True Story*. London: W. H. Allen, 1978.

Battersby, H. F. Prevost. *Man Outside Himself*. London: Psychic Book Club, 1943.

Bennet, Glin. *Beyond Endurance*. London: Secker & Warburg, 1983.

Bennett, Gillian. *Traditions of Belief*. London: Penguin Books, 1987.

Besant, Annie and C. W. Leadbeater. *Thought-Forms*. London: Theosophical Publishing Society, 1905.

Bozzano, Ernesto. *Phénomènes de bilocation*. Paris: Leymarie, 1937.

Caidin, Martin. *Ghosts of the Air*. St. Paul, MN: Galde Press, 1995.

Cave, Janet, Laura Foreman, and Jim Hicks (eds.). *Hauntings* (Mysteries of the Unknown series). Alexandria, VA: Time-Life Books, 1989.

Coghlan, Andy. "Midnight Watch," *New Scientist*, Vol. 160, No. 2165/6/7, Dec. 19/26, 1998–January 2, 1999.

Cohen, Daniel. *The Encyclopedia of Ghosts*. New York: Dorset, 1984.

Colombo, John Robert. *Mysterious Encounters*. Willowdale, Canada: Hounslow Press, 1990.

Daniels, Pat (ed.). *Phantom Encounters* (Mysteries of the Unknown series). Alexandria, VA: Time-Life Books, 1988.

David-Neel, Alexandra. *With Mystics and Magicians in Tibet*. New York: University Books, 1956.

Defoe, Daniel. *The apparition of one Mrs. Veal, the next Day after her Death, to one Mrs. Bargrave, of Canterbury, the 8th of September 1705*. [Popular booklet of the period.]

Defoe, Daniel [writing as "Andrew Moreton"]. *Secrets of the invisible world disclos'd, or, an universal history of apparitions sacred and profane, under all denominations; whether Angelical, Diabolical, or Human Souls departed.* London: J. Watts, 1735.

Evans, Mayme. "I never flew alone," *Fate.* May 1969.

Faill, Bill. "UFO car-napping in Rhodesia," *Fate,* January 1977.

Flammarion, Camille. *Death and its Mystery: Volume 2: At the Moment of Death.* London: T. Fisher Unwin, 1922.

Freixedo, Salvador. *El diabolico inconsciente,* Mexico: Editorial Orion, 1977.

Garrett, Eileen J. *My Life as a Search for the Meaning of Mediumship.* London: Rider, 1939.

Goss, Michael and George Behe. *Lost at Sea: Ghost Ships and Other Mysteries.* Amherst, NY: Prometeus, 1994.

Green, Celia and Charles McCreery. *Apparitions.* London: Hamish Hamilton, 1975.

Guiley, Rosemary Ellen. *The Encyclopedia of Ghosts and Spirits.* New York: Facts on File, 1992.

Gurney, Edmund, Frederic W. H. Myers, and Frank Podmore. *Phantasms of the Living.* London: Rooms of the Society for Psychical Research, 1886.

Haining, Peter. *A Dictionary of Ghosts.* London: Dorset, 1982.

Hardin, Terri (ed.). *Supernatural Tales from Around the World.* New York: Barnes & Noble, 1995.

Harris, Melvin. *Sorry—You've Been Duped.* London: Weidenfeld & Nicolson, 1986.

Hauck, Dennis William. *Haunted Places: The National Directory.* New York: Penguin, 1996.

Holzer, Hans. *Ghosts: True Encounters with the World Beyond.* New York: Black Dog & Leventhal Publishers, 1997.

Hufford, David J. *The Terror that Comes in the Night.* Philadelphia: University of Pennsylvania Press, 1982.

Imich, Alexander (ed.). *Incredible Tales of the Paranormal.* New York: Bramble Books, 1995.

Inglis, Kim and Tony Whitehorn (eds.). *Ghosts and Hauntings* (Quest for the Unknown series). Pleasantville, NY: Reader's Digest, 1993.

Ingram, John H. *Haunted Homes & Family Legends.* London: Gibbings, 1897.

Innes, Brian. *Ghost Sightings.* New York: Barnes & Noble, 1996.

Jaffé, Aniela. *Apparitions and Precognition.* New York: University Books, 1963.

Jarvis, T. M. *Accredited Ghost Stories.* London, 1823.

Lukianowicz, N. "Hallucinations à trois," *Archives of General Psychiatry,* 1959, 1, September.

MacKenzie, Andrew. *Adventures in Time: Encounters with the Past.* London: Athlone Press, 1997.

MacKenzie, Andrew and K. M. Goldney. "Two experiences of an apparition," *Journal of the Society for Psychical Research*, Vol. 45, No. 746, December 1970.

Mamontoff, Nicholas. "Can thoughts have forms?" *Fate*. June 1960.

Matthews, Robert. "Science finds a sound reason for ghosts," *Electronic Telegraph*, Issue 1129, June 28, 1998.

Morley, L. Collison. *Greek and Roman Ghost Stories*. Oxford: Blackwell, 1912.

Natsis, Carol and Merl Potter (eds.). *Almanac of the Uncanny*. Sidney: Reader's Digest, 1995.

O'Donnell, Elliot. *Twenty Years Experiences as a Ghost Hunter*. London: Heath, Cranton, 1916.

Podmore, Frank. *Telepathic Hallucinations: The New View of Ghosts*. Halifax: Milner & Co., 1909.

Podolsky, Edward. "Have you seen your double?" *Fate*, April 1966.

Pugh, Griffith, quoted in editorial in *Fate*, August 1971, page 25.

Ross, Catrien. *Supernatural and Mysterious Japan*. Tokyo: Yenbooks, 1996.

Spencer, John and Anne. *The Encyclopedia of Ghosts and Spirits*. London: Headline, 1992.

Tyrrell, G. N. M. *Apparitions*. London: Duckworth, 1943.

Underwood, Peter. *A Host of Hauntings*. London: Leslie Frewin, 1973.

Vandendorpe, Laura. "Ghost Hunters Link Data with Unexplained Images," *R&D Magazine*, Vol. 40, No. 7, June 1998.

Warren, Joshua P. *Plausible Ghosts*. Ashville, NC: Shadowbox Publications, 1996.

Wilson, Colin. *Poltergeist*. St. Paul, MN: Llewellyn, 1993.

Wilson, Ian. *In Search of Ghosts*. London: Headline, 1995.

RESOURCES

If You Should See One . . .

♦ Don't panic. Ghosts are not frightening unless you allow yourself to be frightened.

♦ Don't look on ghosts as something evil to be "busted." Some of them may be malevolent, but they have no power over you unless you allow it. You are living, they are not (usually).

♦ Don't contact the media unless you have personal acquaintance with someone who will give your ghost serious attention. Generally, any attention you will attract from the media is likely to be of the worst kind.

♦ Don't call the police. This isn't their line of business. It's no crime to be a ghost.

♦ Do make notes, as detailed and as comprehensive as you can, of your experience. Who saw what, when, where, and how. Check times and measure distances. Obtain independent accounts, if there are any, and don't compare notes till you've written your accounts. Get every witness to make a sketch, regardless of their artistic skill: it could contain valuable information. Do this as soon after the incident as you possibly can.

♦ Do contact experts, if you can find them. (Some addresses are given below.) But remember: many of these organizations are concerned primarily with establishing the truth about what happened. Be prepared to have the experience, which seemed so amazing to you, explained as something not quite so amazing after all.

UNITED STATES

American Ghost Society
515 East Third St.
Alton, IL 62002
Phone: (618) 465-1086
Website: *http://www.prairieghosts.com*

American Society for Psychical Research
5 West 73rd Street
New York, NY 10023
Phone: (212) 799-5050 Fax: (212) 496-2497
Website: *http://www.aspr.com/index.htm*

Ghost Research Society
P.O. Box 205
Oak Lawn, IL 60454-0205
Email: *DKaczmarek@ghostresearch.org*
Website: *http://www.ghostresearch.org*

International Ghost Hunters Society
12885 SW North Rim Rd.
Crooked River Ranch, OR 97760
Phone: (541) 548-4418
Email: *ghostweb@ghostweb.com*
Website: *http://www.ghostweb.com*

International Society for Paranormal Research
P.O. Box 291159
Los Angeles, CA 90027
Phone: (323) 644-8866
Email: *Ghost@hauntings.com*
Website: *http://www.hauntings.com*

The Office of Paranormal Investigations
P.O. Box 875
Orinda, CA 94563-0875
Phone: (415) 553-2588
Email: *esper@california.com*
Website: *http://www.mindreader.com*

GREAT BRITAIN

Association for the Scientific Study of Anomalous
    Phenomena (ASSAP)
Postbox 327
Bromley BR1 1ZE England
Email: *research@assap.org*
Website: *http://www.assap.org*

Society for Psychical Research
47 Marloes Road
London W8 6LA England
Phone/fax: 44(0)20-7937-8984
Website: *http://moebius.psy.ed.ac.uk/spr.html*

CASE INDEX
Arranged by date

October 21, 1972	*West Point, New York*	*50*
1974	*Yonkers, New York*	*100*
1975	*Roebourne, W. Australia*	*116*
September 1975	*Culver City, California*	*52*
1976	*Hong Kong*	*54*
1977	*East Anglia, England*	*102*
August 1977	*Hammer Springs, New Zealand*	*28*
March 31, 1978	*Uniondale, South Africa*	*56*
July 1978	*Bridgewater, Canada*	*124*
August 25, 1979	*Sarmiento, Patagonia, Argentina*	*58*
Fall 1979	*Old Washington, Ohio*	*60*
October 31, 1980	*Kawasaki, Japan*	*62*
May 20, 1981	*Palavas-des-Flots, France*	*104*
Summer 1981	*Edmonton, Canada*	*134*
Late 1981	*Salem, Massachusetts*	*64*
December 8, 1983	*Dublin, Ireland*	*126*
July 1985	*Cheltenham, England*	*66*
June 4, 1989	*Madrid, Spain*	*68*
1990	*Marin County, California*	*118*
July 5, 1991	*Gettysburg, Pennsylvania*	*30*
November 8, 1992	*Kent, England*	*70*
Mid-1990s	*Erie, Pennsylvania*	*128*
May 5, 1995	*Hope, Derby, England*	*72*
November 1995	*Scappoose, Oregon*	*74*
December 1995	*Tuzla, Bosnia*	*86*